Kathy

you are SO loved

xo

i

Fireweed

I am His Fireweed, blooming
from adversity, a display of his splendor

Jennifer Mae

Fireweed

ISBN: 9781085811903

The publisher, author, editor, translator, transcriber and/or designer disclaim any liability for loss or injury resulting from the use or interpretations of any information presented in this publication. No liability is assumed for loss or damages resulting from the use of the information contained herein.

This book is not meant to promote adoption as the only or best option or represent adoption as a whole.

I have tried to recreate events, locations and conversations from my memories of them. In order to maintain their anonymity, I have changed the names of individuals and places, I may have changed some identifying characterizes and details such as physical properties, occupations and places of residence.

All scripture quotations, unless otherwise indicated, are taken from the Holy Bible, New International Version®, NIV®. Copyright© 1973,1978, 1984, 2011 by Biblica, Inc.™ Used by permission of Zondervan. All rights reserved worldwide. www.zondervan.com. The "NIV" and "New International Version" are trademarks registered in the United States Patent and Trademark Office by Biblica, Inc. ™

Cover Design: Jennifer Mae
Cover Photo: Matthew Thomas
Author photo: Matthew Thomas

For my Boogaloos. Do you have any idea how much I love you?

For my Sweet Man. I love the life we have worked so hard to build together. Moreover, I love you.

Table of Content

Introduction

Fireweed is a beautiful pinkish-purple flower that takes root in the ashes after a forest fire. If it weren't for the ashes, there would be no exquisite fuchsia beauty.

In order to flourish, I had to suffer the flames. This is the memoir of my fire and ash; this is God's story of redemption and beauty.

Blessed is the woman who is covered in floured hugs and tiny sugary kisses.

Blessed is the home whose walls echo boisterous giggles and whispered I love yous, and whose floors shake under dancing feet both big and small.

Blessed is the world by the children raised in and by love.

Chapter 1

One of the Best Days of My Life
Present Day

The sweet warming smells of melted butter and pure vanilla extract fill my kitchen and overflow into the adjacent dining room. Standing by the weathered, cherry stained dining table, surrounded by a tornado of toys, books and stuffed animals, are two curious, yet innocent eyes peeking over the top of a green sippy cup lid. The corners of my mouth turn up into a soft smile as I think to myself how much I love that tiny person with the delicate blue-grey eyes.

I had dreamed of my daughter for so long. In my mind's eye I had pieced together a picture of a little girl that looks just like me; thick locks of deep brown curly hair, large doe-brown eyes and rosy cheeks.

Other than her stubborn personality she did not inherit any of my features. Not that I was disappointed that she looks like a miniature, softer, more girlie version of my husband—I thought it was sweet—she just was not the picture I had drawn up in my head, but she most certainly was the dream I had prayed to come true for so many years.

The just over two years since my daughter was born have been heart-aching, stressful, joy-filled, nerve racking and *so* wonderful. Two years of a mind full of adjectives and a heart full of emotions.

For many years prior to my daughter's birth, my heart longed and prayed, not only a child, but for a girl, a daughter of my own. Do not get me wrong, I have had my fair share of feeling overwhelmed with the culture shock of having your first baby at home, post-partum depression in the early months and then the sassiness and messes that a toddler can bring. But all that never made me forget how immensely blessed I am to be her *mommy*.

I made the choice to recite to myself in the midst of those frustrations a child can bring,

"Even in the stress, whines and sass the blessing to be a mommy greatly does surpass." [1]

Sure, there were times that I had to repeat this phrase more than I would care to admit but being frustrated and overwhelmed does not an ungrateful mother make.

You see, when a deep seeded yearning for a child is bestowed upon your heart and is watered for years with your cries of longing, you prayerfully hope for a child that will be not only physically present in your life but bring forth the long-awaited joy of such a unique relationship. Truly, the blessing to be a mommy outweighs the stress of sleepless new-born nights and tantrums of a two-year-old.

I had lived for years with an ache in my heart for a child; I knew the sorrow of longing for even the not so great days that a child can bring. But even though tantrums and whines are inherent with child rearing, I would not trade my worst days as a *mommy* to live life without the (usually) sweet, blue-eyed babe-child God blessed me with.

---

[1] See, "Poem for my Baby Jane" on page 202.

"I prayed for this child, and the LORD has granted me what I asked of him."

- 1 Samuel 1:27.

The perfect verse to describe my tiny love—the Lord heard my longing prayers and blessed me.

As I look at my heart's prayer manifested before me, surrounded by an explosion of mess, I softly whisk the ingredients in the paisley bowl resting on my hip. My mouth still turned into a soft smile, as I begin to daydream on the past and how such a tremendous blessing was granted unto to me.

Daydreaming

For many people, the day their child was born could be counted as the best day of their life. Not for me. It was not that my labor was so difficult, because as far as the worst physical pain a woman could endure, it really was not that bad. The best day of my life was when I got into the hospital wheelchair and held *my* baby, I was wheeled down the hallway, put into the elevator with *my* baby in my lap and my husband at my side. I was taking our daughter home.

Although that is not an insignificant event in parents' lives, it is really never mentioned by parents when asked, "What was the best day of your parental life?" Typically, this question conjures up answers of, "The day she was born." But usually not, "The day we left the hospital."

Although, I am sure those who have struggled through having a baby in the NICU would share my joy in leaving the hospital, but I digress.

Regardless of the standard answer, I did not have to think the first time I was asked this question. And, to this day, I still get teary-eyed when I think about the day I brought Kaylin Jane home. Tears well, as I know what it is like to leave the maternity ward without joy and without a child...

"The most beautiful people we have known are those who have known defeat, known suffering, known struggle, known loss, and have found their way out of the depths. These persons have an appreciation, a sensitivity, and an understanding of life that fills them with compassion, gentleness, and a deep loving concern."

Elisabeth Kubler-Ross

Chapter 2

The Worst Day of My Life
January 15th, 2002

Eight years prior to Kaylin Jane being born, I had left the labor and delivery floor, exhausted physically from bring forth life and drained emotionally, though the hard and heavy emotions from new grief had only just begun.

This bone-chilling, heart-aching day was truly the worst day by far, although it was followed by many consecutive horrible days.

Unlike my best day, when I left the hospital in 2002, I left without my baby in my arms, nor husband by my side. I was wheeled down the hospital hall, pushed into the elevator, as I uncontrollably sobbed for the child that was not with me, and I went home with nothing but my grief and my parents to accompany me.

I gave birth to my daughter, whom I had named Siri many months prior to her birth, on January 12th at 8:04pm. She was so beautiful; olive skin, thick brown curls, chubby rosy cheeks and she had my large doe-shaped eyes, yet her irises were blue, unlike my or her biological father's brown. Sure, most all babies are born with blue eyes, but Siri's eyes were such a bright blue that one could argue she would most certainly keep her inherent pigment.

Beside me during delivery was my dear, sweet Mother. She, along with my Father, were disappointed that I was unwed, seventeen and pregnant, but they supported me all the way though, which to this day I am still immensely grateful for. At the other side of the hospital bed, holding my hand was Siri's Mother…

"Loneliness and the feeling of being unwanted is the most terrible poverty."

Mother Teresa

Chapter 3

Telling My Parents
May 2001

I appreciate that you are probably deeply wondering who my child's other mother is, and not appreciating the delay in clarification, but to justly explain, I need to go back a bit in this daydream to when I was newly pregnant and in the car, heading home from my high school with my mother.

My mom had come to pick me up because I was sick. It was morning sickness, but I had not told her this, although I am sure she already knew. I had been acting strange around my parents, hiding my face as to not let them see my fear and constant puddle of tears in my eyes, but staying close because I was terrified and so, so badly needed someone in the corner.

"Jenn." My mom paused her words for a brief moment as she continued to drive home.

"Are you pregnant?" My mother asked sternly, yet with tenderness in her voice.

"I'd rather answer that when Jeri (the biological father) is with me."

She said nothing, keeping her eyes forward on the road. I saw her through my peripherals, but I was too terrified to turn and fully look at her and to hear what she was going to say next. She took a long pause, I am sure, to let my words sink in, and then she looked at me with eyes full of sorrow and tears overflowing down her flushed cheeks.

I could tell that she was disappointed and upset, but she did not yell. I do not remember her exact words because I was too terrified at the time to retain what she said, but I do know that she was calm and she was kind, not giving me the verbal lashing I thought I so deserved. I know now that my Mother acted in the grace and mercy of God. She loved me *unconditionally*; she still showed me love in the midst of being disappointed, angry and hurt.

I was not expecting that reaction from her and looking back I believe I appreciate it more now that I have my own child who tugs at my heart strings from time to time. I understand that my mother put her hurt and anger aside and allowed God to take over which is not always easy to do as a parent. She could have yelled, she could have belittled me for my choices, but she showed me mercy.

Agape. It means a love not based on feelings, rather, a love based on self-sacrifice. This is the love that Christ had at the cross and the love my mother showed me this day and many days thereafter.

The rest of the ride home was filled with long pauses and the occasional question my mother would think to ask. Questions like, "How far along are you?"

...backing up time a bit more to answer my mother's question...

I was in my car in the back, wooded, undeveloped part of my neighborhood about three weeks prior to my mother asking me this question. It was late; the only light was a streetlamp that I parked near, but not too close as to avoid drawing attention. I got out of my car walked around to the passenger side and opened both doors to conceal what I was about to do. I unwrapped the pregnancy test, squatted and then after the five seconds of squatting that the test required, I replaced the cap and got back into the car. I was so sick to my stomach; I knew what it was going to say, but I tried to convince myself that *maybe* the tiny window would read "not pregnant." The longest two minutes of my life, waiting for the test to complete were finally up. I picked up the test and my heart started to pound even harder behind my labored breath. The test confirmed what I already knew by my late period— I was pregnant.

Yes, this was not the most dignified way to take a pregnancy test. But, being that I did not want the possibility of my parents finding out, I had to do it in a place that I would be least likely to be found, and so, my teenage brain with my still developing prefrontal cortex (the part of the brain that has to do with planning and reasoning among other functions) thought to take shelter in the privacy of the back woods.

…back to the car with my mom…

"I'm not sure." I responded to my mother's question. Which, truthfully, I really did not know exactly how late my period was and the exact date I took the pregnancy test. My mind was filled with more panic and fear than dates and facts at this moment. And so, giving a full explanation to my mother was not something that I could put into complete thoughts, let alone articulate in words during that drive.

We finally arrived home, I went to lie down on the couch, and she went to tell my father the heart-breaking news.

I was thankful that she told him, that I did not have to go through telling him myself. I felt like a failure, ruined and unworthy. I was convinced my father would only confirm my feelings and I could not handle hearing him belittle me because I already felt so small.

You see, my father is the product of parents who had strict gender roles, which he carried into his own family life. His mother was the nurturer and his father was the breadwinner and there was absolutely no overlap of those gendered roles.

Growing up I did not know that my father was out of his element, per say, when it came to showing affection and spending quality time on a *child's level*. I read his lack of affection and intentional time as something being wrong with me; because he rarely *chose* to spend *quality* one-on-one time with me and when he was in my presence, he was easily angered, I internalized that as I was not a likable person.

Children often see their parents as blameless, so when a shortage occurs in some area of their relationship, the child often places the blame on themselves. For me, I saw my father's parenting style as his choice to escape my company. I felt he did not care for me as a person, thus chose to spend long hours at work and was irritable when he arrived home, not because of his stressful, hard worked hours to provide for us, but because he was angry that he had to be with me.

Young children, developmentally, can only think in concrete concepts and it was a very concrete notion that when my dad was around me, he was livid and annoyed but when he was with his coworkers, other family members and friends he was a happy, fun-loving, outgoing man. Seeing that he was capable of being all those wonderful things, just not with me, was further reassurance to my immature mind that I was despised by my father.

My father was mirroring his parent's parenting in the way he was raising me. It was a parenting style that worked quiet well on him which is why he continued it into his own parenting. He viewed the father's love being shown through providing, that his hard and long hours away at work and his paycheck was his nurturing and his anger to my rambunctious child-like playfulness was coming from his desire for me to be a calm and gentle lady of great character. But I needed him to show me affection through physical touch, quality time and not try to parent me into a different person but accept me for the person God created me to be, while also parenting me to be a better version of the woman God placed in his care. Being that I was a little girl, it was hard to articulate those feelings and being that he was a man taught to not show affection, we were constantly on two totally different paths.

My path, unfortunately, was that of feeling disliked and unworthy of a man's affection. I desperately needed to be validated by my father, to be shown that I am a likeable person and worthy of affection. Being that I was not getting that at home, immature and unable to articulate these feelings, I turned to the world to find out how to get the feeling of being worthy of love.

The world's view on a woman's worth is her sexuality and as a teen I dove in because it felt so good to finally be seen, heard, "valued" and "loved". And that is how I got to be in this position of overwhelming fear of rejection in telling my father I am pregnant.

Laying on the couch my stomach turned from morning sickness and fear of my father's reaction. I did not fear him kicking me out of the house, I could not see him doing that to me. I knew he loved me, but I also "knew" he did not like me, so my fear was rooted in him using me as an emotional punching bag for his stress and anger in my choices, which ironically, my choices were engrained in him using me as an emotional release for his stress and frustrations from work.

As you can imagine, I was surprised that when he was told of my pregnancy, I was not given the verbal pounding I thought I deserved and could have sworn he was going to give me. Yes, he was disappointed, and he was upset, but he did not raise his voice and he did not make me feel small. With tears in his eyes he talked to me with the love and mercy of Christ, just as my mother had.

After processing the devastating news, my parents tried to tell me that I had to place the baby for adoption. I had done my research previous to them finding out. I knew that they had no legal control over what I chose. This child was under my custody, not theirs, even though I was a minor. I had weighed my choices previous to this moment and had already chosen adoption for my baby and me. Being that my choice was made, this was my reply to my parent's recommendation, and I can still picture standing in our family room telling them this, "What I choose is adoption, because I chose it, not because you suggested I should. I view it like a beautiful painting in a museum. Each brush stroke is exquisitely thought out and given to the canvas through the artist's own mind and heart, not by someone giving painting instructions to the artist on how to bless the world with their art. I too, am going to be a blessing to this child and her adoptive family and I need you to understand that *I* need to be the artist of my own canvas."

I was stubborn to a fault as a teenager, absolutely hardheaded to the point of it had to be my idea for me to do anything with any sort of haste or enthusiasm—this is what I meant by my daughter inheriting my stubborn personality. Ugh. Ha-ha!

But when I do have an idea, that is my own, I run with it; I pursue it to its full extent. And therein, adoption was my idea that I would take to the ample end.

Yes, I knew early on that adoption was right for my baby and me. That does not mean it was an easy or rash choice. In fact, it was the hardest choice I have, or probably ever will make. But I knew in my heart that it was for Siri's benefit and I loved her enough to put her well-being ahead of my desire to parent her.

I needed my parents to support me, but not push me, to guide me, but not force me. I knew this was going to be difficult, that I initially would have no control over the pain that was to come flooding in after I placed Siri; the pain that only a mother who has lost her child can completely understand. Once my baby was gone, knowing it was *my* choice to have her go to a different life would be one of my few strongholds that I would so desperately need.

My parents were supportive, not just at this time, but the whole way through, and even to this day. Even though my father and I had our hardships, I am so grateful that he and my mother were the ones there for me in my greatest time of need.

(Present day, I am tearfully happy to say that my father has asked for my forgiveness for the way he treated me when I was young. His sincere apology is also tethered to action, as he now sees my need for his affection, and though it is still out of his element to do so, he makes a tremendous, intentional effort to speak my love language. I, likewise, put forth an effort to understand his roots and his own love language. Additionally, he is a playful, funny, patient, kind man who appreciates me for the attributes God *did* give me and no longer treats me as though he is disappointed and angered that I was the one born to him. Whereas, we did not have a healthy relationship when I was young, we currently have a wonderful relationship that is built on the foundation of forgiveness, respect, love and empathy. It is still a work in progress on both ends, but my father recognizes my need for him to show me love through hugs and quality time spent together and I see him as a whole person with history and depth.

Between the two of us being intentional, we are building a bond I have always longed for and needed with my dad. And, if all that healing, forgiveness and coming together was not enough, the sweet man has even humored me and taken the Enneagram personality test to further understand how God made us individually, as for the two of us to have better relational health.

My father and I do not share the same number on the Enneagram; I am the Helper, type Two, a relationally driven person, and my father is the Perfectionist, type One, a goal and betterment driven person. Current day my dad is a healthy type One—a good man of great and noble character, seeking God and working hard to be the man God intends him to be by loving well and serving others well to bring about a better world. His One-ness truly shows in his drive to achieve the goal of a better relationship with me. My relationally driven type Two personality is in health, especially because this extremely important connection with my father is being nursed in a fashion that I have needed all along.

Understanding the Enneagram has led me to recognize, in my adult life, that I am a likeable, loveable person despite what I was shown and taught as a child.

An unhealthy type One, according to Ian Morgan Cron and Suzanna Stable in the book, "The Road Back to You", "fixates on small imperfections. These Ones are obsessed with micromanaging what they can. Asserting control over something or someone is their only relief."

Learning this as an adult brought me so much peace and gave me the ability to take the titles I had placed on my father's shoulders, titles like, "tyrant" and replace them with grace. My father was not trying to communicate that he despised me. He was trying to find relief from his overwhelming stress from work by attempting to make me perfect in his One processing and coping mind.

He was unhealthy, not a tyrant.
And, it was never that I was or am an
awful, unlikeable, unworthy human being.

I wish I could go back in time to whisper this to the little girl aching for relationship, longing to be shown that she is not loathed nor worthless. But that wishful thinking will not change my past but learning that my worth is in Jesus and gaining the ability to place grace where titles once reigned certainly has changed my present and my future.)

Before I get back to the memories of my past, I want to take and moment and speak to those who are parenting in the present. I hope this chapter speaks to your heart. I pray you know how deeply, passionately and profoundly important you are in your children's lives. I cannot stress enough that each child is their own fearfully and wonderfully made individuals. Get to know your children on a deeper level; I encourage you to learn your and your child's Enneagram number and unique love language and speak that language to them daily. Not only will your children benefit from having their cups overflowing with love, but you will benefit from a deeper relationship with the people God chose to bless you with, which will allow you to speak God's truth and love into their lives in a way that your children can comprehend.

> *"Love the Lord your God with all your heart and with all your soul and with all your strength. These commandments that I give*

33

*you today are to be on your hearts.
Impress them on your children. Talk about
them when you sit at home and when you
walk along the road, when you lie down
and when you get up. Tie them as
symbols on your hands and bind them on
your foreheads. Write them on the
doorframes of your houses and on your
gates."*

- Deuteronomy 6:5-9

God calls us—not explicitly Mothers nor specifically Fathers, but parents as a whole—to speak the love of God on our children. The verse says,

> *"...talk about them when you sit at home,
> as you walk on the road, as you lie down
> and as you get up".*

-Deuteronomy 6:7

In every aspect of our lives as parents God tells us to speak the love of and for Him on our children. In order to speak this love, we must, as the verses say, spend time with them.

God has given me this beautiful depiction of tying the commandments to our hands and binding them to our foreheads. This visual God placed in my heart is of a parent wrapping their hands around their children and placing their foreheads on their shoulders. I see arms eagerly ready and abundantly willing to embrace our children in a hug and a rested forehead placed close to nestle the love in deep. Words can be challenging for kids to understand, but words along with tangible examples—physical touch (hugs), quality time (on a child's level)—is what children need to apprehend loving with all their heart, soul and strength.

For fathers to *only* be the breadwinners, I believe is a vast shortcoming to attaining what this scripture calls us to do. Most children do not understand that money equates care, that is a very mature beyond their years concept and further, monetary provision is *not* a love language. If we want our children to understand love and understand a loving God, we must show them what love is, on their level. To know that level, we must know our children and to know our children we must spend time with them.

The following is something absolutely key to loving our children well and I have prayed over these following words for myself and for those whose hearts need to hear this;

It is a hard concept to learn that a Heavenly Father loves you, cares about you and desires a relationship with you when you feel like your earthly father does not.

That seems like a huge, pressuring undertaking, but I do not mean that fathers need to be their children's God. Just by loving our children well, our children can see more clearly how a big God could possibly care to love them and be in a close relationship with them.

My father did not show me that I was cared for outside of monetary provision and worthy of a relationship with him when I was young (again, he is currently a changed, healthy man). But there is no gain in saying, "If he had only taken the time to know me and love me well, I would not have looked to be known and loved by a man in the wrong places". There is only gain in using my past to bring hope and healing to others; to speak for children who do not have the words to express their ache, who long and need to be seen, known and loved well by their parents. And there is gain in helping parents, like me, to break the cycle of hurt from the generations before.

As you continue on with this book, I am prayerful that through my heart in words you see women in crisis not merely as their choices and current circumstances. I was not simply an un-wed pregnant teenager. No, I was so much more than the surface of my expanding belly. I was a girl longing for love from my father. I was hurting and unaware of what authentic love was and desperately searching for the broken relationship of my youth to be healed. I searched for that healing and I found what I did not recognize as a broken, emotionally abusive relationship with a man who had no intention of bringing me the healing I so desperately needed to be a happy, healthy, relationally driven Two.

"You are not a victim. You can control your reactions. You do have a choice."

Dr. Caroline Leaf

Chapter 4

The Biological Father
May 2001

When I told Siri's biological father, Jeri, I was pregnant and thinking about placing our child for adoption, he made the choice to not be involved. Looking back, I am glad for that, although at the time it hurt beyond words to hear him say that I am being selfish to him and his mother for not aborting the baby. Then to be abandoned by the man who I thought loved me, cared for me and fathered my child when I refused to comply with his attempted *manipulation* was difficult, to say the least.

That was Jeri in a word—manipulator. When we started dating, he slowly, but meticulously guilted me into cutting off my friendships, making him the only one I had in my immediate circle. He would manipulate me into his will and belittle me into nothing more than a sex object that was flawed—according to him—in a few key areas. Jeri would speak to others about my physical "flaws" and thereby shamed me which further produced the feelings of being "lucky" to have someone willing to lower themselves to love me. Shame produced gratitude and gratitude produced further fondness. I was so broken from my unhealthy relationship with my father that belittlement, to me, was a sign of love.

My father never belittled my looks as Jeri did, but he did unintentionally demean my personality. I heard often as a child a singular, three-word response followed by an invisible locked tight, sole key bound wall on any further communication on my plead for him to hear me. "You're too sensitive", my father would state after I would pour my heart out to him in attempt to heal our relationship, in effort to get him to see how his treatment of me was hurting me so greatly. Those three gnashing words recited to me, accompanied with his barricade in place on further communication started to transform as the years went by.

My father's words went from the concrete meaning in childhood to the interpretive meaning in adolescence, "You're too sensitive", my father would deliver, but the father of lies would latch onto my thoughts. "No, no child", the devil would whisper into the open wounds of my brokenness, "He's not treating you in any other way than you deserve. You aren't worth of his kindness; you aren't worth his time or his relationship, nor anyone else's. You are worthless."

I know now that my father's upbringing and unhealth in his One-ness at the time caused these words and actions as I stated in the previous chapter. But as a child I internalized and grew around my father's picks and prods of my Two-ness.

I, perhaps, was *too stubborn* to give up on our relationship, so I continually came to him with how he was impacting me in hopes to heal our relational unhealth. I was, maybe, *too determined* that he was capable of being the wonderful man he is today, but I was not, "too sensitive". Nonetheless, my knowledge now was not known then and thus as the years went on into my angsty, broken state of adolescence I was an easy target for a manipulator like Jeri.

I honestly felt that Jeri cutting my friendships off was him showing me that I was funny and smart in my conversations to the point that I was ultimately worthy of being around. I was so emotionally broken from my father attempting to make me "perfect" and not allowing me to have a healthy relationship with him, that I was an easy game to the first man that made me feel worthy of this time and likeable enough to be around.

I assumed the focused, flaw-pointing, sexual attention I was getting from Jeri was love. I did not recognize that what he was doing was mentally and emotionally abusive and physically using me. My eyes had only begun to open to all the wrong he had done to me when he ran off to another state to be with another woman soon after I told him I was pregnant. My heart, already broken, withered in despair at his abandonment. Yet again, the father of lies was happy to speak into my brokenness, "You are replaceable, you are unworthy. Your father despises you and so does the father of your child. See, I told you that you are nothing more than worthless".

You may think I am stupid for allowing myself to be treated so poorly, but I was so broken that abuse resembled love. I was fourteen years old when Jeri and I started dating, just a child, but I had so many years of neglect and blatant emotional disregard under my belt that I was ready and willing to do whatever it took to remove that taxing emotional weight.

My heart withered and my thoughts wallowed in my unworthiness, but as I earlier specified, I was glad to not have Jeri involved in this pregnancy. Had he been involved he could have tried to stop the adoption, but because he had not supported me either emotionally or monetarily during the pregnancy, he had no parental rights because he had abandoned his child and me. Consequently, according to state law, I did not need his permission to place my daughter for adoption. I knew adoption was the best parenting plan for Siri and me, so to dodge that potential roadblock to placement really was a blessing in a nasty, heart-breaking, tear-jerking, pit-in-your-stomach disguise.

(I want to make sure I am not building fear of biological fathers in the hearts of those choosing to adopt. I do not want to leave the impression that *all* biological fathers are like Jeri, because they most certainly are not. Men are capable of being nurturing and desiring to parent or lovingly and thoughtfully choosing to place their child for adoption. But in my case, at that time, that was not true of the man who fathered my child. So, while I speak of my fears, heartaches and concerns it is not to build those emotions within others, it is to justly explain my schema and choice for adoption.)

I feared that Jeri would try to stop the adoption just to punish me. In that I mean, I feared that he would contest the adoption, force me to parent and then abandon Siri and me again.

Keeping Siri would not be the punishment, she is not a consequence. The punishment would have been the abandonment and the emotional and financial struggle to follow, which both Siri and I would have felt that trauma deeply.

I could mark off multiple checks on the A.C.E. (Adverse Childhood Experiences) test, adding poverty and feeling mentally and emotionally incapable of taking care of my own child, while struggling through the normal stresses of parenting, was not another trauma that I wanted to add to my accumulating sufferings and, with great conviction, not one I wanted Siri to be impacted by either.

Jeri did return while I was pregnant, months after he had abandoned Siri and me. I naively decided that I would give him another chance, to see if he had actually changed and was capable of empathy and support. I do not know if Jeri had ended the relationship with the woman in the neighboring state that he ran to when he left me or if he had remained with her and merely came to visit his parents. Regardless, when he asked, I agreed to meet with him.

I went to his parent's house and from there we got into his truck and he started to drive down the country road adjacent to his home. I am not sure where we were heading—I do not remember that—but I do recall that we did not get far before I asked to be taken back to my car so that I could go home.

"Whoa! She is *SO* hot!" Jeri said with a foul delight seeping from his lips.

He was gawking at a woman bending over in the parking lot of the tiny hole-in-the-wall diner a short distance from his home.

Here I was, scared, obviously pregnant with *our* child, and emotionally raw from his previous words and actions, yet I was gracious enough—or stupid enough, either way—to give him another chance.

I felt a knot in the pit of my belly after he spoke those words of lust towards another woman. He had abandoned me physically months prior for another woman, now he was in full disregard of my emotional needs.

His gross, objectifying words hurt but showed without a shadow of doubt that he had no empathy or support in his mind or heart for me or the precious being I carried in my womb. Though emotionally wounded, my mind was clear in that moment and I was able to stand up for myself in asking to be finished with this atrocious get-together.

I did not want this life for myself and surely, not for my daughter. She deserved a dad who was wild about her, eager to spend quality time with her, build her up emotionally and mentally and show her how important, loved and worthy she is. I saw that Jeri was profusely not that man for her and made this the last time I ever saw him by choice.

Yes, I was abandoned and treated poorly by Jeri, but I have forgiven him for that, and harbor no ill feelings towards him. I sincerely hope that he finds the ability to forgive himself, to be able to live a life free from guilt and full of happiness. I truly hope he finds Christ.

It took me a long time to get to this place of forgiveness. Had you asked me years ago if I hope he is happy, healthy and able to forgive himself I would have replied with something spiteful and bitter. But, over the years, coming into a deeper relationship with Christ, I have found that I am forgiven by God. If Christ can forgive me for my transgressions, who am I to withhold forgiveness from others who have wronged me? Jeri's actions, though I do not know this for certain, were likely rooted in his own hurt. People who are hurting tend to pour that out on others. Whether Jeri poured hurt onto me with malicious intent or because he was spilling out what his heart was overburdened with, I do not know. But my forgiving him is not contingent on ever hearing him apologize, getting retribution or knowing where his behaviors were coming from, because my forgiveness of him was coming from the overflowing mercy that was bestowed to me by God.

In saying all this about my relationship with Jeri, I am not trying to paint myself as a victim. I was a teenager who made a mistake. I am accountable for my actions leading up to pregnancy, during and after, just as Jeri is. Nor do I want you to think that I blame my father for my actions. I merely want you to see the importance of my circumstances leading up to my pregnancy and my choice for adoption.

Most, dare I say, all, little girls do not grow up thinking, "Oh, I hope I can place a child for adoption when I grow up." A back story occurs for adoption to be the chosen parenting plan, circumstances are in play, history and environment matter.

I am not a victim, but I had no responsibility over how others acted and their own personal choices. My responsibilities lie in my response to others around me and my choices in my environment.

I metaphorically envision my responsibilities this way; I chose to cross the street without deliberately looking for danger. I had carelessly opened up a senecio where I could get terribly hurt by not being intentional with my heart nor my body.

Sure, one could say that I was never taught to look both ways before stepping out into the road (what a healthy relationship looks like). But I still had the responsibility of taking those *rushed* steps out into the street (into an intimate relationship with a man that did not cherish my heart, mind, body or soul).

I did, in my negligence, get struck by a vehicle (I did get wounded by Jeri). I was at fault for allowing myself to be in a situation where I could get hurt, but the vehicle striking me (Jeri belittling and abandoning me) was not my responsibility. My actions leading up to the crash and the healing thereafter, those were my responsibilities.

I had the duty of picking myself up from the wreck, dusting myself off and working astronomically hard to heal my wounds and obtain a different life for myself and my daughter. I took all that hurt, anger and loss from that horrendous crash and filtered it through my innate motherly drive to protect my child; to place her into the safety of a home well-equipped to teach her about her *intrinsic value*, her *right to healthy boundaries*, exhibit to her *safe relationships* and authentically *love* her without naïveté of any of the above.

Before I go on, I want to make myself perfectly clear with this; my actions were a mistake, but my daughter *never* was a mistake, she never will be, and she never could be. She was created *when* I sinned, not *because* I sinned. When is only a time, not a reason; she is not a product of sin. Sin does not have the power to knit life in a mother's womb. She is alive because God called her to life. Siri is the fearfully and wonderfully made creation of the Heavenly Father who claims her as His beloved child.

Though Siri's earthly, biological father betrayed her and did not value her, her worth was always inherent because of who her Heavenly Daddy is.

I want you to understand that I did not make my adoption decision rashly; I wanted my child with every fiber of my being. But I was only sixteen when I found out I was pregnant and incapable of adequately caring for an infant. And, quite frankly, Jeri was not willing or able to be a dad. Siri deserved a father that loved her and spoke that love to her daily. From what I understood at the time, Jeri would not have provided her with what I believe little girls desperately require, what they deserve from their dads. I knew, on a small scale, the pain of longing for love to be tangibly shown by my father, I did not want Siri to go through that hurt. (Though, I now understand her loss of Jeri and his abandonment of her in the womb could still equate that sorrow. And there's the rub...)

At that time, adoption is what I viewed as my responsibility; to put my daughter's greater good over my desires to parent her and to have her close, by physically removing her from the repeating ache of a father who chooses not to show up, love deep and place her above narcissistic pursuits. And remove her from a mother who was not mature in her own knowledge of her own inherent worth, right to healthy boundaries and intentionally seeking safe relationships. By placing Siri into the loving care of a man who is ready, willing and able to be her father and a woman who is mature in her mental and emotional life, I did what I viewed as a greater chance of a successful, healthy life for her.

All this is not to say that single parents are inherently bad for choosing to parent without a healthy, present parenting partner, nor am I trying to communicate that single parents and those with mental illness are incapable of being effective parents. I am merely speaking on my own thoughts concerning my own time of crisis and how I personally handled my responsibilities and coped in my environment to give my daughter and myself a different life.

To hit home why I was not able to parent Siri as she deserved, I am going to be candid in a way that does not make me look good. This book is not a vain pursuit of my self-glorification; I wrote it to bring healing, empathy and understanding for those who are widely stigmatized and disenfranchised (birth/ first/ biological parents). But none of those righteous pursuits can manifest without my vulnerability.

I did not meet up with Jeri at this time for any other reason than to validate my own worth—to ease my derivation wound. It was a very self-serving pursuit, especially considering I had the fear of Jeri contesting the adoption in my mind. The pattern of hedonism, of seeking my

51

worth in worldly terms, was not easy to break. My daughter deserved a mom who did not put her selfish chase to ease her wounds above her daughter's well-being.

I am not advocating that I should not have placed my own mental and emotional health in high priority—just as the flight attendants tell us to put the oxygen mask over our own faces before helping others, I needed to address my own issues before I could address Siri's needs, before I could effectively parent her.

One pours from their cup what it is filled with. My cup was filled with stress, sadness, anger, unhealed wounds, poor self-esteem and depression. Absolutely, I needed to administer self-care to refresh my proverbial cup, to be able to care for others around me in a way that poured joy, love and encouragement over them. But at that time, I did not know what *healthy* self-care was, I just knew that old habits added a momentary drop of bliss to the ick that encompassed my cup.

Thankfully—as odd as that is to say—Jeri stopped adding short-lived sweet and only added to my overflowing ick with his vile words of lust.

I think him showing me my old ways would no longer work to relieve some of my pain and stress nor boost my self-esteem, was what allowed me the courage to ask to be returned to my car.

In that moment I had—for what may be the first time in my life prior to this instance— administered healthy relational-self-care by creating a healthy boundary in breaking close ties to unsafe relationships. It was not perfect, I was not perfect (nor am I now), but I was on my way to emptying my cup of all the awful and filling it with God's intended goodness for me, to overflow from my cup onto those I do life with and the pages of this book.

Again, to stick with the candidness, even if Jeri was kind to me and did not acknowledge the attractiveness of another woman when I am physically and emotionally aching with pregnancy, I would have chosen adoption anyways. It was the best thing that I could have done for my daughter given my circumstances and my own mental state. She deserved more than what Jeri was willing or able to provide initially and at the time of the adoption and more than what I was capable of providing.

I was not capable of providing but choosing adoption does not make me a bad mom. I think many people have this incorrect connotation of parents who place their children for adoption; that they all are bad parents dumping their kids off into other people's care. But not all birth moms are bad parents—and not all birth dads for that matter. They are parents that see the inadequacies in their environment and their inability to amply provide in some fashion or another (e.g. the inability to fully provide emotionally and/or monetarily in their current circumstances) so they bravely lay their desires to be a "mommy"—or "daddy"—and lovingly and self-sacrificially place their child into the care of parents and environments more well-equipped—*from loving arms to loving arms*. Placing a child's needs over a parent's desire is being an excellent parent, not a bad one. One does not need to place for adoption to place a child's needs over their own desires, but in my case, I viewed adoption as the best course of action for me, as a loving parent, to provide my daughter with a different life than the one I was suffering through.

Briefly, I want to mention the parents who have their children taken from them by C.P.S. and have their parental rights removed, thereby attaining the unchosen title of birthparent. This source to attaining said title does not always mean that these parents did not try to provide more for their children than what they were shown and given in their own childhood. We can choose to place labels on these men and women, labels like drug addict, or we can choose to place grace instead. Grace that sees things like drug addiction as, perhaps, a coping mechanism they learned or were taught in their youth and physical neglect as the only parenting style they themselves had ever been shown in their adolescence. My point is, adults in their shortcomings do not just appear, they are created overtime. Not to say the children in these homes should not be protected, *absolutely* they should, but we can protect and lay down grace, it does not have to be either/ or, rather it can be both/and. Because in that grace, we can build healing, rather than shame.

The thing is, parenting is hard, placing a child for adoption is hard and abortion is hard. It is all about the hard that you want to face in an unplanned pregnancy. No matter the choice we make—and we do have the choice to choose what hard path we will walk—that hard path at some point will require us to acknowledge it and work through it. Even if you choose abortion so you will not have to face your hard path, I truly believe you will have to face it at some point. Whether that facing be intentionally processing or through life bringing you to a boulder in the road that forces your feet onto the path of acknowledgment.

I chose to face my hard path head on; to admit the short comings in my environment and as a parent. I chose to acknowledge that every life is ordained and to work hard to give the wanted, loved child called to life in my womb the greatest chance at health and happiness that I thought I possibly could, given what I had to work with intrinsically and extrinsically.

Adoption is not for everyone. I truly believe God calls those in unwanted or mistimed pregnancies to either parent or place, but each person is uniquely created to walk a distinct hard path with Christ, even if that path is first chosen in their own fleshly fears. As long as we as parents seek God's will in our journey down our chosen hard paths, we can acknowledge it and intentionally walk down it without ever being alone and with the promise that we are redeemed in Christ's care, though we may still flounder or fall as we make our way.

This is where I want to be clear on where I stand in my faith and love for people. I will only speak on this for brief moment, so, please, do not give up on this book. I believe you will miss so much of God's redemptive story is you walk away now.

I wholly believe that the mother who chooses abortion is forgiven when she turns from the world and seeks God's forgiveness. Just like any other person who has fallen short of God's glory, which is every single person in the history of ever, except for Jesus Christ.

> *"But God demonstrates His own love for us in this: While we were still sinners, Christ died for us."*
>
> *-Romans 5:8*

Shaming the mother who had an abortion—using religion as an "ordained calling" to back up hateful words with the intent to disparage these women into a relationship with Christ—is not living and loving in the image of Jesus, nor will it bring these women to the feet of the cross.

Jesus conversed with, ate with and befriended the people who were actively sinning. He forgave their sins when *they came to Him* and *willingly* humbled themselves to ask for His mercy and forgiveness.

The religious people of Jesus' time hated Him for associating with the sinners. But we all have fallen short, and beyond that, those who have come from the most destructive of flames often make the deepest contributions to the Kingdom of God—the most vibrant and deeply rooted of Fireweeds.

You may have heard the old saying that God does not call the qualified, He qualifies the called. Well, what if we really believed that and lived that out loud? What if we saw all people as Christ does as they are being refined for His calling? This might be hard to hear but this is where maybe we need some heart work; God loves the abortionist, those who get abortions and those who support abortions. He loves them just as much as the child in the womb and those who are fighting to end abortion.

A sin like hating someone for their choices may seem like a lighter weight of depravity than abortion to many of us Christians, but all sin is the same swing velocity of the hammer atop the nail head that hung Jesus to the cross. I believe it is righteous anger that we have towards innocent children being slain but using that anger as a fuel to hate the abortionists, the mothers who choose abortion and those who fight for pro-abortion policies is not bringing about life in the wombs or hearts of anyone, Christians included.

Can you imagine how many more lives we could help plant into Christ's grace and how many less abortions we would see if we loved unconditionally the baby in the womb just as much as the mother carrying the child, the staff at the abortion clinics and those shouting for things we do not agree with? I am not saying that we

58

should enable sin, or not stand firm in the truth, but see the person God loves, not purely focus on the anger for the particular sin the person is doing. I get Holy Spirit chills when I visualize us, as a people of God, living for and like Christ in seeking out the hurting, befriending the active sinning (with healthy boundaries) and showing them how Christ can bring forth great beauty even from the most horrendous of ashes. A present-day Saul to Paul redemptive narrative for our nation[2].

I can earnestly tell you that if I did not go through the fires of unplanned pregnancy and adoption I would not be refined for His calling.

I was like iron, steadfast in my stubborn, hedonistic, sinful ways. Christ knew the only way to sharpen me for His will was to use iron just as hard as my self-indulgence. Iron that took the shape of an unwed pregnancy, abandonment of the biological father of my child, placement of my birth child and the ultimate grasp to God that I desperately required to be able to take root into God's vast field of grace and grow into something beautiful rather than remaining in my self-destructive blaze.

---

[2] Saul was a murderer of Christians until God transformed his heart (and his name to Paul) to be a great disciple of Jesus. Acts 9:1-19

My mother loved me in this unconditional way. She saw me at my worst, yet treasured me despite her anger towards my sin, but she also held strong to God's truth. She, sometime later down the road, confided in me this beautiful, love filled, heart-breaking prayer she took much time to muster the courage to bring before God while I was in the thick of my flames;

> "Lord, whatever your will, *whatever it takes*, bring my daughter back to you."

I can only imagine the hurt that had to cause my mother in feeling the desperate need to pray that over my life; that my life had gone so far away from God's will that she finally let go of what little control she felt she had over me and gave me to the Lord in prayer.

"Whatever it takes."

My Mother loved me enough to pray for God to smolder my self-destructive flames and to give me His beauty instead of my ashes. God loved my mother and I enough to answer...

Jeri. Manipulator. Abandoner. Answer to a sincere cry of a Mother's loving prayer.

"For where two or three gather in my name, there am I with them."

Matthew 18:20

Chapter 5

The Profile
July 2001

About six months prior to delivery (ah, delivery, where I was with Siri's other mom—I have not forgotten. This is all relevant and I *will* come full circle, I promise. Please just stay with me as we jump around a bit in my memories) my mother and I met with an adoption coordinator, Helen Trymann.

Jeri was long gone at this point, so he was not there to meet Helen or support the adoption process and my father was at work, but he was supporting my mother and I through his prayers.

We met Helen for the first time in a tiny booth at a restaurant that no longer exists. Following behind the hostess to be seated next to this stranger that I was about to pour my heart and soul out to made me feel quite uneasy. She was in the business of making families and my initial understanding of adoption coordinators was that they favored the adoptive mom and looked down on the expectant mom planning to place their child. Sure, no one told me this to be true, but I felt like a failure, unworthy of love, so how could a complete stranger look at me, a pregnant teenager, in any other way then through sin tinted glasses...

Helen's face was adorned in large blonde curls, her mouth turned into a welcoming, genuine smile and her eyes, her eyes were a vibrant, beautiful sky blue; I know this because she looked at me without the barrier of sin tinted glasses. She was warm and welcoming, never once during this first meeting—or any time after—did I feel anything but compassion and understanding from her. She was a very kind woman with a heart for God who helped Christian families adopt, and expectant families find Christian parents for their babies. My initial understanding of adoption coordinators was laid to rest with her; she did in fact care deeply about adoptive couples, but she made me feel like I was her priority, she made me feel worthy and lovable during a time that I felt like neither and made sure to reassure me that I was in control of my adoption plan and that if I ever felt the desire to stop the plan and parent, she was one hundred percent on my team and would make it all go away. I felt so much comfort in knowing that Helen was on, "Team Jenn", she was rooting for me no matter my parenting choice and was there to assure my choices were established and honored.

Helen had brought a slender, well dressed woman with her to this first meeting. Jane, a birth mom herself, was there to answer any questions I may have that only someone in my position could wholly answer. It made me feel more at ease to have Jane there with us. I felt like a failure, like I was surrounded by people cloaked in purity and I was drenched in sin. To have someone there with me that was not perfect and could empathize with how I was feeling made me feel like my round, swollen, "scarlet A" belly was not as defining of my inward character. As I mentioned, Helen did not ever once make me feel unworthy, but when you have this view of yourself being mule in a room full of horses, you *feel* different and a little dirty, even if the horses do not treat you like anything but their own kind.

Helen pulled a total of eight family profiles, all candidates for parenting my child, out from the canvas bag that laid at her side. I flipped through the pages, reading the biographies of each family asking for the sacred honor of being able to raise my baby. Some were couples longing for their first child and other were already established families, but all had a picture in their best dressed, Sunday clothes and the biggest, liveliest smiles. "We do this, we like that, we, we, we..." Every profile was dedicated to the family's biography; meticulously describing themselves, never once stopping to take a breath to recognize the person on the other end of this ordeal.

As I looked through the biographies Jane reached across the table laid her hand down and touched the picture on the page I was on.

"That's my son," she said through a smile, without her voice quaking, or tears flooding her eyes. The adoptive parents of her son were looking to add another child to their family.

I remember that so vividly because I saw this woman, she had been through the hell that I was in, and here she was, on the other side of placement, smiling and talking about her birth child without sorrow, shame or regret. She was there to make me feel more at ease and to answer my questions, but Jane was there for a much greater God appointed reason—to show me the tear and voice-quake free joy that I could have eventually after I placed my child in the loving arms of a Christian family. Pain and sorrow are in adoption, absolutely, but Jane showed me I would not be forever immersed in that overbearing heartache.

Helen had told me I could take any profiles home I liked so that I could have more time to think about whom I would choose, but I knew instantly which family I wanted.

The one and only profile that really stuck out to me was the woman I chose to be at my bedside, holding my hand while I brought forth *our* daughter. (I told you I did not forget about Siri's other mom, but we're not quite back to the delivery room yet, bear with me.) I chose her, her husband and their daughter—also adopted—because of the opening lines of their adoption profile, which none of the other profiles mentioned until the end of theirs;

> *"First off, <u>God Bless You</u> for considering making this difficult decision. It must be the largest and hardest decision of your life. Your decision to place your baby with a family who will love, care and nurture him or her is <u>abundantly unselfish</u> and it shows a great deal of love."*

The Lovettes were the only profile that immediately acknowledged I existed beyond giving them a baby, my baby. Not that the others did not mention me and their gratitude towards my potential placement with them, but their acknowledgment was to be found in the last paragraph. Almost an afterthought, though I am sure I was not an afterthought. But when you have found yourself sixteen, pregnant and abandoned by the father of said child, it is so easy to read the negative in places it may not be.

Theodore Roosevelt was right—

"People do not care how much you know until they know how much you care."

This quote rang true for me in my adoption story. That's not to say *all* women choosing adoption have my same mindset, I am not *all* birth moms, but this whole book is laden in my perspective as that is what I am an expert in and have found *some* other women do, in fact, feel the same as I do.

You may think my reasoning is selfish, but I needed to know that I was important, that I was not just an incubator. I needed to feel loved by Siri's family, cherished for what I was going to do and not forgotten once they have her. I surely did not want them to agonize over me; I did not want them to look at Siri and see me in her and therefore feel *guilty* for having her. I just needed them to understand the magnitude of what I was going to do – the courage, love and total selflessness that it was going to take; I needed to be acknowledged. And for Siri, I needed them to know that she was losing her first family. I needed them to grasp that deep and hurtful trauma of losing your roots so that they could be the best parents for her. Being able to acknowledge and honor me, in my mind, equates them being able to acknowledge and honor my daughter's mental and emotional health. Our culture has this incorrect notion that adoptees should be *only* grateful for their adoptive parents "saving" them. I needed to know that they would not stifle Siri's hard potential truths. That they would honor her primary loss—the loss of me, her birth grandparents and truthfully, her birth father as well. Some may be thinking that I was too young to process this way but being that I have adoption in my extended family, I knew a bit more about adoption than one who has had little exposure. Not to say that my family has ever communicated a loss or trauma, but that I felt that for them even before I myself became a birth parent.

The Lovette's profile spoke to my heart in a way that made me feel seen, loved and like I was not just the means to their end—like I was more than an incubator—but a girl who would grieve deeply after they had Siri. Like Siri was not merely the baby to fulfil their dream and asphyxiate their infertility grief, but a valuable human with her own thoughts and feelings that needed to be honored, nurtured, healed and loved.

Though I did not know the Lovettes by merely looking at their profile, I felt an instant connection and told Helen that I wanted to meet them to further confirm this is the right family to raise my daughter.

"There is no fear in love. But perfect love drives out fear..."

1 John 4:18

Chapter 6

Meeting Siri's Parents
August 2001

I met Siri's adoptive parents, Annie and
Lucas Lovette, minus their daughter, Lillian, for
the first time at Helen's house. My mother and I
arrived there before them, so we would not have
our initial meeting in the driveway, but in the
comfort of Helen's home and the ease of her
presence to help guide the meeting in a smooth
and pleasant way. We were escorted to the
formal living room to sit and wait for the Lovettes.
I was so nervous; I placed my shaking, anxious
hands in my lap, clenching them tight as to slow
the trembling. Inside my head a thousand
thoughts impatiently danced.

"Should I hug them when they come in or wait until they leave? Will they even want to hug me? Should I risk them awkwardly pulling away from me when I tried? Will they like me? Will they look at me with condemning eyes because I had so clearly had sex outside of marriage? "

Finally, after what seemed like a hundred restless hours—it was only ten minutes in real world time—the potential mother and father of my baby rang the doorbell. All of me wanted to jump up, run to the door and swing it open, but instead, I nervously kept my seat.

Annie came and sat next to me. She did not touch me; I am assuming because she had my very same thoughts. She did not know how I would react. Her blue eyes were puddled with tears and her mouth was turned into a downward smile. At this moment all my worries and anxieties about the Lovettes dissipated.

Annie did not look at me like I was ruined, like I was a sinner. Instead, she looked at me like I was her light of hope; like I was an angel of God, sweetly and lovingly bringing cherished life into the world. She looked at me with hope, but she also looked at me with sorrow. She seemed to know that I was a girl with feelings, a girl who would not disappear once she had my baby, if I did choose them. She knew what it was like to want a baby with every ounce of her, but not being allotted that dream. She knew that her potential blessing was my pain and it showed so clearly on her face.

The way Annie carried herself and the way she treated me was so graceful. From her compassionate expressions to her thoughtfully cautious body language, from her gentle voice to her loving words; it all beamed with kind, affectionate love. An instant bond was formed, a connection I would later come to find I would instantly have with most Christian adoptive mothers. This connection goes beyond the outward appearance—a shared experience in adoption—and into a true deep sisterhood, a real love and respect that is mutually shared between Christ-following birth mothers and adoptive mothers.

I have focused in on Annie, Siri's Mother, but I want to acknowledge the key role that Lucas played in choosing this family to parent my child. Lucas was mostly quiet during our meeting, but he had a calming, kind presence about him. The way he looked at Annie with deep, loving eyes, the way he let Annie go first through the front door and be the first to sit. I noticed those things and appreciated how he honored her. He seemed to give her a great deal of respect and empathy, which I could only imagine must also trickle-down to Lillian and soon, to my daughter too. In their profile Lucas had mentioned that he coached Lillian's sports team and that deeply struck a chord in my heart; a father who is willingly involved on a child's level. That is exactly the type of father I wanted for Siri.

As you may have suspected by this meeting and the previously mentioned presence of Annie in the delivery room, we wanted to have an open adoption. Our specific title for the relationship that our triad would hold was, "semi open" as we planned to have contact before I delivered, during delivery, but not any physical contact after I placed Siri for adoption.

I matched with the Lovettes after this meeting, meaning I wanted to place Siri with them, and they wanted to parent Siri. Being matched does not mean that I was not able to change my mind and parent Siri; the adoption choice was not final on my end until, at least, seventy-two hours after birth. The match meant I was given the time to get to know them and lay out our expectations of what our relationship would look like after (and only if) I choose to follow through with placement and signing a Termination of Parental Rights (TPR). Some in the adoption world believe that matching expectant mothers with hopeful adoptive families is unethical as it can be seen as coercive. I greatly believe as a birth parent that matching before birth allowed me the opportunity to get to know the people who I would be placing my child with. Had I not been granted the chance to get to know them I would have been riddled with anxiety over who my child was going home with. Matching gave me, as a protective momma, the chance to verify over the course of time that the character of the people I chose was authentically good and safe and that they truly did desire to give Siri the best they could.

During my pregnancy Annie showed me her good and safe character by writing me letters filled with empathy, asking about my health and happiness, and the baby's well-being. Their three-year-old daughter, Lillian, would color me pictures and I would receive store bought cards filled with handwritten well wishes from them during the holidays. These greetings and well wishes were sent to the adoption coordinator, Helen, who acted as a liaison as to keep the arrangement *semi* open. That was exactly what I needed; to be shown that they were safe and that I mattered through this all. When I received these precious pieces of mail, I would sit alone in my parents' formal living room, rip open the envelopes and read, trying to picture how great a life Siri was going to have with Annie, Lucas, Lillian and all the extended family they had pictured in their profile and spoke so highly of during our first meeting.

It was at this first meeting that Annie, Lucas and I agreed that for the first two years of Siri's life they would send pictures and letters telling me about the milestones she hit and the overall welfare of the family. Knowing that I was not being cut off cold turkey from my daughter, that I was going to be able to see a small portion of her (hopefully) great life with her loving, compassionate, Christian family made the worst day of my life a tiny bit bearable.

Back when I placed it was not known that open adoption was the healthiest route, or best practice, for the adoptee, adoptive parents and birth family. This is not to say that my adoption agency failed me and my child—they were so, so good to us. Culturally speaking though, open adoption was not something that was remotely common practice or widely known in the adoption world to be best. If I could go back and advocate to have a continued relationship with Siri after placement—had I of known it was best for her mental, emotional and physical development to not fully lose her roots—I would have been there in a heartbeat, but at that time open adoption was not how it is today. Pictures and letters were given to help the birth/ first/ biological family grieve, but not done with the adoptive parents or adoptee in mind. Yes, I understood Siri's loss of me would be hard, but as most did, I thought that would be combated by counseling and adoptive family support, not an active relationship with the birth family encompassing healthy boundaries, clearly communicated expectations, open communications, intentional time spending, forgiveness and grace.

Annie and Lucas did very lovingly offer to let me see Siri for one more time after the adoption was finalized—when Siri would be six months old. At that time thinking about saying goodbye forever for a second time was far too agonizing and so I declined the meeting. I could let that haunt me, I could be stuck in the "what if they let those meetings continue" and "I should have said yes". But I did not know then what I know now, and so, I must take those thoughts captive and filter them through what is true (I did not know) and what heartache does not strain through the truth, I must nail to the cross, as to not let the devil have the power of finger pointing and belittling me for being human in my knowledge base.

" And the peace of God, which transcends all understanding, will guard your hearts and your minds in Christ Jesus."

Philippians 4:7

Chapter 7

Peace in The Midst of Chaos
November-December 2001

As the months of my pregnancy moved forward with the Lovettes checking in on me (and Siri) from time to time through written word, we approached December. My loving mother took me to a Christmas store just before December first. She bought me a tree full of beautiful white and silver blown glass ornaments embellished with silvery gems and sparkles, strands of diamond-like radiant Christmas lights, a breathtakingly beautiful angel with feathers, pearls and fiber optics and iridescent garland. It all was absolutely gorgeous. I think my mother knew that I needed some quiet beauty in my life, a place to sit and be so overwhelmed with soft light, splendor and a symbol of God's undying love and care for us; even in the dead of winter the evergreen tree remains steadfast and vibrant, a mirror of its creators character.

My mother saw me through this whole pregnancy and recognized that a peaceful, beautiful tree would bring me some joy in this sorrow filled season. She not only supported me in my choice to place for adoption and in trying to make me feel better, but she also supported me through taking me to my doctor appointments, making sure I ate a well-balanced diet with the occasional weird craving—prune filled cookies are *not* as delicious as my hormones had me believing previous to the first bite, and on that note she held my hair back as I crouched, heaving into the toilet from morning sickness. She was my emotional support when I needed to vent, cry and just simply have someone be present in my struggle. While I know I was the main sufferer in this story I also saw my mother tirelessly laid her hurt and suffering down to be my support. That is truly a depiction of my mother, unselfish giver of empathy and time. She is a Nine on the Enneagram, truly a peacemaker able to empathize better than most.

My mother and I together put up the over-the-top, elegant tree in the formal living room of our home on Goldpine Court. White lights made the already gorgeous ornaments come to their full potential of beauty. The angel adorned with a soft fiber-optic glow looked down sweetly from the top of the tree adding to the overall peace and beauty. Whilst pregnant, next to this tree of peace and beauty is where I read my letters from Siri's potential adoptive parents and where I also wrote a journal, which I will get to later in my story. I felt peace from knowing I had chosen the right family to adopt Siri—the peace that only God could give—and the peace I felt from the quiet beauty of the Christmas tree—this selfless gift my mother gave me to tangibly show me how loved and cared for I was through all my heartache and grief. This is why I love Christmas so much; in that time of my life I was scared, stressed and over-burdened but, by that tree, God granted me such a sense of overwhelming peace. Even in the chaos that life now brings around the Christmas season with a child of my own, to this day,I find peace when I sit near the soft glow of the white lights of the very tree my Mother gifted me with many years ago.

I knew I wanted to place for adoption, and I knew without a shadow of doubt that I was going to follow through with my choice, because I had been given such a gift. Not the tree, but I was granted the blessing of my mother, the greatest support God could have given me in my time of need. Because of my mother I was able to know and follow through with my plan. Without her I would have struggled ten-fold to place Siri. Please do not get the impression that I felt coerced by my mother to place. She supported *my* decision. She was there for me, not to see that I followed through on *her* choice. My mother was God's gift to me, my peace in the midst of chaos, my precious, empathetic Nine.

God's love and plan for me is far greater than my past misinformation or present disappointments.

Chapter 8

The Journal
December 2001

"*I am placing you in the loving, capable arms of your adoptive parents because I want you to have a different life than I can provide you with. I am only seventeen years old and thus, I feel that I cannot take care of you the way you require and deserve. Please know that I want you with every fiber of my being, but it is that very same love that desires to keep you that acknowledges my inability to give you the life I believe you deserve in my current circumstances.*"

I wanted Siri to know that she is so loved, so wanted by her birth mother that she would never feel insecure in her worth. I did not easily give her a different life through adoption, and I needed her to know that; not for selfish reasons, but purely for her own mental and emotional health when she gets old enough to begin to question. I have heard from more than one adopted adult in a closed adoption that they struggled with insecurities, feeling unwanted and unworthy and having abandonment issues. I wanted to make sure Siri never felt that way because she was not secure in knowing her birth mom loved (and still loves) her and placed her with the hopes to improve her life and well-being, not to get rid of her. I know that Jesus Christ is the only one in whom we can find our worth in, but that concept is hard to grasp when you feel discarded and unwanted by someone close. A reality that I understood all too well, though I myself am not an adoptee.

Sitting by the peaceful light of the Christmas tree I wrote Siri passages about how I felt and how I love her. I also put pictures of me, my family and yes, her biological father, Jeri.

Jeri chose not to be involved in my pregnancy, but he was involved in her conception. Siri's genome was (and is) fifty percent him. I knew Siri would be curious, I knew she would want to know what he looks like, so for her benefit I put his picture in. I did not mention that he was not there or anything of the harsh words he chose to speak or his failed manipulation, I merely placed a picture of him in and wrote who he was.

My very last words on the very last page of Siri's journal:

> *"When it comes time that you are able to find me, my arms are open wide waiting for you, but if you do not, I will know your life is so full that you did not need me in it. I pray that if I do not meet you here on Earth that someday I will meet you in Heaven. I love you."*

Some of you may be confused that I did not say that I would come find her. But the truth is, at that time, I felt that I did not want to disrupt her life. I do want to be a part of her life. I so badly want to wrap my arms around her, squeeze her tight, and tell her, "Do you have any idea how important you are to me? Do you know how much I loved you and still love you?"

I had hoped in telling her, "I will know your life is so full that you did not need me", would relieve her of any guilt she may feel from not coming to meet me, if she so chooses not to find me. At the time that I wrote that journal, I believed that if she does not seek me out that she is living a life so full of love and satisfaction that she just does not feel the need to have me in her life.

Present day, with all my training to become an adoption assessor and college training, specifically in psychology, I have come to find out that I had illusions of a fantasy in writing that journal excerpt. Her life is not guaranteed to be beautiful, whole or better just because she does not seek me out, nor because of the parents I chose, or that I physically removed her from the hurt I foresaw her suffering in staying with me. I do not have a responsibility *for* Siri—it is not my job, nor can I save her from any sort of strife she may be walking through emotionally because of my placement of her—but I do have a responsibility *to* her.

I have given much thought to reaching out to Annie to let her know that I am willing and able to answer any questions she, or Siri, might have as pertaining to Siri's placement and/or roots, but I am still in the works of praying that over. If I do reach out, that is not a part of the story I would likely share, as it is not mine to tell. My thoughts and feeling, desires and pursuits pertaining to my environment and placement are mine to share. But intimate details of Siri's story after I placed her for adoption are not mine to tell. I believe that if Siri wants that part of her story known, she should be the one to share it, not me. But I will say this, I have a derivation wound of my father not showing me love in the way that I needed and I truly believe it was not my responsibility as a child to ask my parent to notice me, spend time with me and love me where I am and for who I am. So, knowing this hurt, how am I to expect my birth child to take on the responsibility of searching for me and asking for my attention and love. Though she has had my love and thoughts all along, she does not know that; what a heartache to not know you are seen, treasured and loved by your (birth) parent.

If I am totally honest—and really, I have not held back so far, so let's do this thing—present day I have searched Annie, Lucas and Siri out online and found their social media profiles and went through all their pictures that they had not marked private. We live in a world of social media, so a true, one hundred percent closed adoption does not actually exist. A mother being curious and seeking out tangible proof that their child is okay is really not shocking. I needed to see that Siri was safe, healthy and loved, but I also wanted to have healthy boundaries in not contacting the Lovettes through a "back door". I put up this boundary because adoption is truly about the well-being of the adoptee. Siri may not be mentally or emotionally ready to open a relationship with her birth mom in these tender years of monumental psychological, physical and

91

social changes. If I do decide, after much prayer, to reach out, I would do so by contacting Siri's primary caregivers, the ones who know what Siri can mentally and emotionally handle. And I would do so in a more formal avenue than social media, like the agency I placed through.

The internet would make contacting the Lovettes so easy, but another reason for my caution, and consequent prayers, over contacting them is that Siri never had a choice in any of this. I chose to place her for adoption, I chose her parents, her parents chose her. For me to take the choice of her being the one to initiate contact, or not, away from her is something I wrestle with and have not fully come to terms with. I want to completely honor her by placing her choice in this matter in high priority, but I also do not want her to think that I have not spent her lifetime loving her, missing her and praying that she is healthy, not only physically, but emotionally as well.

For the time being, every so often I check in on Siri to see how she is doing, also understanding that social media is not a whole nor, perhaps, even true depiction of her real life. So, prayers still flood my heart that any of her sorrow through her adoption can sit next to and not swallow whole any of her joy. I have prayed that her sorrow is being honored and she is able to speak the truth of her grief and not made to feel that she cannot share her hard emotions. Along with that prayer of peace in the heart of my birth child, prayers of discernment of God's will in me reaching out to Annie also quietly cry out to God.

For another layer of honesty, in more of my internet searches, I found out that Jeri was accused of committing a rather malicious crime that he was arrested for, though I am not sure if he was convicted; I did not care to follow the case as it weighted too heavy on my heart. I ached for Siri and for Jeri. I pray that Jeri has changed, not only for Siri's benefit—I want her to have a contented and healthy relationship with him in the future if she so chooses to find him, or if he becomes curious to seek her out—but, also for Jeri's benefit. Yes, Jeri caused me so much hurt and trauma, but I serve a God who is greater than any hurt, trauma or sin. I pray that Jeri comes to know Jesus so that he can be a safe person for Siri, but also, so that he can spend eternity in the presence of God.

I am fully aware that I am praying for the man who abandoned and betrayed me to dwell in 'my Father's house' where I will be also when the Lord calls me home. If Jeri does ask for forgiveness and seeks the Lord sincerely, he will get called by name by the Heavenly Father who created him. Jeri will be redeemed, forgiven and thus cloaked in the purity of the restorative blood of Jesus if he is walking the golden streets. My Holy Spirit earnestly longs for everyone—even those who have hurt me greatly, like Jeri did—to be in the presence of the Lord. My mind cannot wrap around the concept of being *totally* at ease in the presence of the man who hurt me greatly. But my Holy Spirit also speaks the truth of no more pain, no more sorrow, nor tears when we get to Heaven, and therein, the awkwardness of being in the presence of Jeri surely cannot abide in such a holy place.

You now know where my heart was all those year ago when I wrote this journal. You can also see how I have come into new information, along with new prayers; and you can perceive where my heart is present day. So, here is where I ask that you pause for just a moment before reading further. I will not call upon you in this fashion again in this book so, please, do not stop reading if this is uncomfortable for you. I think it is prudent that I ask you to pause and pray for all the people and potential future relationships mentioned in this chapter. Beyond those in my specific triad, I also ask that you pray for all the other birth parents that are heavy-hearted in their concern for their birth child's well-being. If praying is not your thing, please do not feel awkward or judged. I do not have the ability to ever know if you prayed and if I see you in public or private, I pinky promise, I will not ask.

Lay down your desire to save, to advise and control a certain outcome and what's left is the ability to love, listen and empower, and in that order of importance.

Chapter 9

Support and Not So Much
May 2001-present day

I was not alone during this pregnancy, as previously mentioned, my parents were very supportive. Some of my mother's side were emotionally supportive, but I had a few of my maternal relatives tell me that the family I am choosing to place Siri with, that they had never met, will not love her. A very unnecessary and hurtful thing to hear when you are in the midst of making this difficult choice for adoption, but my parents more than assured me, and I believe the Holy Spirit assured me too, that those words were spoken out of good intentions though they were not kind, nor from a place that understood the whole picture.

I believe my maternal extended family members wanted me to parent Siri, not fully grasping the entire situation. But knowing how much they love me and consequently love my daughter caused them to petition for me to keep her. I wanted them to support my choice to place Siri for adoption, not to give me advice on how they would handle the situation themselves. But because I had such a great support system in my parents, I did not feel a huge lack from their choice to not be emotionally supportive.

My one specific family member had fostered children in the youth of her motherhood. She did not feel as connected to her foster children as she did to her biological, so she placed Siri's story in the box of her story of not loving her foster children the same as her biological. It is important to remember that our knowledge and schemas are brought about by our own experiences. Others will have vastly different knowledge and schemas from our own, so to try to fit other people's life experiences into our own is one-sided and critically damaging to the uniqueness of our own stories. I do not believe she was pushing against adoption to be cruel, but she was placing her own experience with non-biological children on *all* those who parent children who do not share their DNA. To assume all adoptive parents do not love their children as much as biological parents do is greatly false and quite sad. I pray that my family member's heart has softened to the truth—that adoptive parents are capable of appreciating and loving their adoptive children with a deep and profound love. In my case, Lucas, Siri's adoptive father, had a deeper and more profound love for his adoptive children than Jeri, Siri's biological father, had for his biological child.

On my father's side, all of my extended family was emotionally there for me, especially my two sweet aunts whom I love dearly, but beyond all that support I had a best friend by my side through it all.

In order to protect all parties involved I have changed dates, names and location, so to continue this path, I shall call this dear friend Jeb, which, very fittingly, means beloved friend.

Jeb willingly gave of his time and energy to not only be there for me during my pregnancy, but to be my much-needed ears for listening and arms for hugging. Beyond that, he allotted me—somewhat—the ability to refocus my mind from fear and sorrow to fun and friendship. He did not take my pain away, but he gave me the ability to be distracted from time to time and just be a teenager. He saw me for me, a seventeen-year-old girl, not just the sin that I had so clearly partaken in.

Having support when you are going through crisis is vital to not only following through on such difficult choices, like placing a child for adoption, but it is essential for healing. If you are close to someone in crisis and you feel that you have the time, energy and resources to say yes to being there for that individual, I encourage you to do so within your God given scope and with healthy boundaries in place.

According to Dr. Henry Cloud, "A boundary shows me where I end and someone else begins, leading me to a sense of ownership. Knowing what I am to own and take responsibility for gives me freedom."

What I believe Dr. Henry Cloud means in this quote, is we *cannot save* people nor make healthy choices *for* them because we are *not* them. There is hard, intentional work in not fully engulfing ourselves within the person in need and the crisis they are in. But that intentional, hard work—boundaries—gives us freedom from any choices that we may not agree with or foresee as potentially detrimental to the person in crisis. Boundaries give us no ownership over the outcome. Having that ownership in the correct hands gives us all freedom.

Just as important, rest assured in knowing that when you set a boundary, that you believe is in line with Christ's will for you, that says no to being the primary support to a woman in crisis, it is not turning your cheek from one of God's people. This type of boundary is knowing where you are useful for God's purpose and not putting yourself in a position where you were not created to help or that will deplete your own mental and emotional health. Another relevant quote from Dr. Henry Cloud is,

"Boundaries help us to distinguish our property so that we can take care of it. They help us to "guard our heart with all diligence." We need to keep things that will nurture us inside our fences and keep things that will harm us outside."

To clarify, I am not advocating for you to not help at all. We were not all called to do the same thing, but we are all called to doing *something*. Linking a family with resources like a Pregnancy Center that will help her make her *own*, best choice and give her a support system through client advocates would be a great way to support her without compromising your boundary. But I want to inform you that while Pregnancy

Centers are wonderful, they often have a hard time talking about adoption as an option. So, finding a reputable, ethical adoption agency who is trained on speaking about this option, without coercion, is also important.

Often Pregnancy Centers not speaking on adoption is due to advocates personal biases and lack of *thorough, continued* training in this area.

The biases I speak of are not originated in the Pregnancy Centers; they are from a culture that views birthmothers and adoption in a poor light. (e.g. adoptive parents are, "Saviors", adoptees are, "Lucky" and birth parents are, "Bad parents". Or, "Children should *always* stay with their *real* parents".)

Pregnancy Centers lacking in thorough training on speaking about adoption stems from, what I assume, is a lack in the budget, not a malicious intent to withhold education. As an example of where staff and volunteers really need a budget designated to more training, often when they hear a client say, "I could never give my baby away." They stop the adoption conversation and move on to another subject, many too afraid or untrained to ask, "Can you talk to me about why you think and feel that way about adoption?" To open the conversation to give clients the opportunity to hear truths instead of the culture full of misconceptions she/they may have walked in with.

Further, I would *love* to tell you to send these women to churches, but often pastoral staff are lacking in knowledge and training in this area and would likely send these women to a Pregnancy Center anyways.

I am not trying to dismiss the value or significance of both resources or state that all centers and churches fall under this category, but overwhelmingly, they do. Rather, I am calling on centers to see the importance of having competent adoption knowledge for their volunteers and staff and the courage to share that knowledge and lay down their own personal biases. I am calling on churches to see the need to be adoption competent, not just when it comes to adoptive families but the mothers and fathers choosing life and the adoptees who are not to be labeled, "lucky" to have lost their birth families.

Why shouldn't these two community resources be ground zero for breaking the cultural stigmas and misconceptions of adoption and the people it encompasses? Join me, please. I, and so many other professional triad-members, would gladly train you!

"It's not how much we give but how much love we put into giving."

Mother Theresa

Chapter 10

Backwards
January 2002

Braxton Hicks came on January 11th, a very cold and snowy evening. My mother and I strapped on our winter clothes and headed out the front door to see if we could walk the contractions into stronger intensity.

When we rounded the end of the street my mother asked me how I was doing. Little to my knowledge that my contractions were only false labor, I asked her to take me to the hospital.

I had mixed emotion about—what I thought to be—my impending delivery. I was so excited to finally see Siri, to hold her and kiss her sweet cheeks, and my body was *profusely* ready to not be pregnant. I was also scared for the physical pain of delivery, but moreover, I was scared for the emotional pain that was looming over Siri's departure from my womb and likewise, my life. My fear did not make me want to stop the adoption; I knew I had chosen the right family for Siri, I had peace about the placement, but I knew that I was going to grieve the loss of her deeply and that knowledge of approaching grief was difficult, to put it mildly.

On our way to the hospital we called my adoption coordinator, Helen, who then called Siri's (soon to be) adoptive parents so that they would know to come. I was admitted into a room and shortly after they told me I was dilated, but not in full labor yet. I was given the option to go home, or to be put on Pitocin. I had heard that Pitocin-induced labor was much more difficult; stronger more frequent contractions which allotted more pain. I knew that Annie and Lucas were on their way. I knew they had a while to drive (although I did not know exactly how long because I did not know where they lived) and that the roads were not great. So, I chose Pitocin. I did not want to make their trip a flop. It was not at all that I thought Annie and Lucas would be annoyed or upset with me, that was not a deciding factor. I do not pretend that I can fully understand the minds of adoptive parents, but from what I do understand from my own view, my pregnancy was their pregnancy in a way—not to diminish my role as Siri's first mother, but I had an appreciation that they would have driven the miles had they been the ones physically pregnant and feeling contractions, so really, I do not believe it was an overwhelming inconvenience to them. I just cared about them and thus did not want to send them home without our baby. So, the hospital booked me and, in the process, asked me about the Father of my child.

I told the nurse that he had chosen to not be involved and I wished to keep it that way as to not disrupt the adoption. I also told them that I did not want my birth announcement in the paper either because I did not want him to find out I had delivered. (Punitive fathers have 15 days post-delivery to contest an adoption in my state; I did not want to give Jeri an in to stop the adoption and abandon Siri and me again.) They processed my paperwork, hooked me up to an IV and I did my best put the emotional pain of Jeri outside my head.

Annie and Lucas arrived in the hospital room with Hellen a short while after I was admitted. The drive was too far for them to come in tomorrow considering I had asked Annie to be in the delivery room during Siri's birth. Annie wanted to be there, but not overcrowd me. She left with Lucas after checking in on me to give me the comfort of sleeping and not feeling I needed to stay awake to entertain their company, but was on call if I progressed beyond eight centimeters so that she could be in the room to see Siri being delivered and support me in the birth.

We said our good-byes and I started to doze off. Hellen turned to my mother before she left with the Lovettes, "If you or Jennifer need anything I am here; I'm only a phone call away."

The night really was not that bad. I was able to sleep most of the night through, only occasionally waking to turn sides to help relieve the small amount of physical pain I was dealing with. My mother stayed at the hospital with me. She, through the whole process, made sure I was never alone.

The next evening the phone call to Hellen was made to ensure that Annie made it in time for Siri's earth side entry. With Annie on one side holding my hand (I told you we'd get here) and my mother on the other, I was well supported and well within the trenches of transition.

I had an epidural, but I had a hot spot—a spot that does not take the epidural so one feels all the pain in that location—on the bottom of the right side of my belly. Yes, I still remember, years later, the exact spot it was because the pain was so overwhelming; I was throwing up, not because I was nauseous, but because my body was in such pain and getting ready to push, and my normally kind personality (according to my mother) was not apparent whilst pushing.

"One more push." My mother would enthusiastically encourage whilst on the first push of a three-push pattern.

Unfiltered, through my gritted teeth, I snapped at her once I had the breath, "Stop saying one more push when I CLEARLY have more than one to go!"

Lucky for me my mother understood it was the pain talking. She did not lash back at my impetuous response to her intended encouragement, but altered her pep talk as to be the best support she could. Truly an Enneagram Nine, my mother is. She is, without question, an irreplaceable blessing. I can only imagine God was there in that room standing with her and whispering His very own words of encouragement into her ears and, perhaps, "Well done, my good and faithful servant."

My body was not that of a child-bearing woman, so after a few hours of throwing up, pushing, tearing, an episiotomy and my mother's encouraging words, the O.B. finally got out the suction cup. It still took quite a few pushes and quite a lot of force on the doctor's end to get Siri out—hello fourth degree tear—but once she was out it was nothing short of amazing. She was perfectly healthy and flawlessly beautiful.

I will never forget Siri's eyes; the whole time she was being examined by the nurses she looked at me, never once breaking her gaze in my direction. The nurses told me that they had never seen that before. I really do believe that was Siri's way of saying, "I love you, mom." This thought still brings me to tears…

After the nurses gave Siri a clean bill of health from the Apgar score chart, they carried her over and placed her in my arms. I held her tight, petting her full head of fuzzy brown hair and kissing her rosy cheeks. The whole time I cuddled Siri, her (soon to be) adoptive mom did not crowd me or make me feel like I could not have as long as I needed to hold Siri. Annie just sat patiently looking at her baby with tears puddled in her eyes. I am sure she was just jumping out of her skin to cradle Siri, but she put me ahead of her wants; I was so thankful for that.

After a few moments had passed, I handed Siri over to Annie. I understood she was not able to have her own children; she had mentioned infertility in her profile. So, my thought was, if I am going to be blessing this family, I was going to go all out, all hands in, knee deep in giving them what they so desperately longed for. So, Annie being there in the delivery room was not something I had to struggle with, or really think about; I knew I wanted to give her the opportunity to experience the birth of our child. Further, how amazing that Annie would be able to give Siri the gift of her birth story. A story that was both beautiful and devastating, all wrapped up in the love for this tiny child.

I was about to partake in the most pain a mother can endure, the loss of her child, but I was not the only one in the room dealing with the devastation. Annie desperately longed for a biological child, but it was not her calling to carry life in her womb. Not that Annie had placed the weight of her loss through infertility on my shoulders, nor that she had not processed her own grief to be mentally healthy for the child she longed to adopt. I just knew from my own experience with adoptive parents that this was a grief they walked with. Like any other grief, we grow around it, but it is not baggage that can simply be put down, but a wound that heals and leaves its scar.

Annie being in the delivery room, seeing Siri's birth, undoubtedly did not take away the pain of not having Siri grow in her own womb and delivering her herself. But I wanted to try to take some of the edge off of going through infertility—not that I had that power, but I still wanted to bless Annie with experiencing birth, even if it was secondhand. Just a few short days later, and many years after that, I would understand the pain of longing for a child with all your heart, a pain that Annie understood all too well and walked with for many years prior to her writing the beginning words on her adoption profile,

"First off, God bless you…"

Annie, the mother of my child, the dear woman whom I chose to be the one who pets Siri's fuzzy hair and kiss her rosy cheeks goodnight, the one who is choosing to nurture what is not hers by nature- first off, God bless *YOU.*

I did not mention to Annie or Lucas that I had named my baby Siri many months ago, while she was still in the womb. I wanted the Lovette's to have control over naming our daughter and I did not want them to feel guilt for not choosing the name I had been using, so I kept it to myself. But I wanted a name for her, rather than "my baby" or "her" or the occasional slip up of "it". I asked Annie what she was going to name her.

"Iris." She said with pure joy in her smile that she tried to hold back from overwhelming me.

She, like I had said before, knew I was not going to stop existing after I placed my baby with her and her family, so she was very cautious about overwhelming me with her happiness of the situation. I felt comfort in her empathy towards me.

Iris... spell Siri backwards and what do you get? IRIS! You can't even tell me that is not a 'God Thing'.

When I heard her say Iris, I felt that God was speaking to my heart, "This is meant to be, you do not need to worry for *I*, your Heavenly Father, have chosen these parents for her." It was like our two motherhoods were mirroring each other in this beautiful reflection of our daughter's name.

I then realized that I may have thought *I* had chosen Iris's family from a profile all those months ago in that tiny booth, but in reality, God chose them, He had just appointed me to find them.

After that profound moment took place Iris's adoptive father, Lucas, came into the room along with my father, my friend Jeb, and Helen. They all got their 'ooohs' and 'aaawws' in and they left to let me rest and have some alone time with Iris.

It was not quality mother-daughter bonding time like you may be thinking. I was exhausted. Too tired to stay awake, my mother agreed to sit by my bedside and watch me sleep with Iris swaddled in my arms. My labor was tiring, I desperately wanted to spend every moment with Iris, but my body's need for sleep overburdened my heart's need for every second with her.

Upon waking the morning after delivery, as planned, Iris's adoptive parents brought their daughter, Lillian, to see me and the tiny newborn.

I wanted to see Lillian's reaction to Iris, to see her in her new role as big sister. Having Lillian come did not make me feel like I did not have the right to choose to parent. In all honesty I knew my choice well and was confident in it, especially after having the wave of peace rush over me in learning Iris's chosen name. But this practice of having potential adoptive siblings come to the delivery room is not something I am necessarily advocating for as this can be coercive for other women in my shoes and distressing for the potential adoptive sibling if the biological mother chooses to parent. But for me in my story, this is what I needed and what I advocated for in my own needs and desires.

In Lillian's petite hand was a brown and green thick woven basket overflowing with goodies. She placed it on the tray next to my bed along with a brightly colored picture that she had lovingly colored for me.

"Oh, Thank you!" I said with wonder.

I was not expecting the Lovettes to bring me anything, as the adoption agency had made it clear that they were not allowed to bring a gift outside of a homemade snack during any of our meetings. The reason being that I could contest in court that I was paid for my child through gifts and then the adoption would be off. Or, I could feel like I owed them my child because they bought me something, and through that coercion, the adoption would be off.

The Lovettes were not paying me for my child, I understood that. They were just being kind and loving. This was just who they were. They could not walk alongside me every day during my pregnancy and they could not be there after the adoption went through, so they wanted to "be there for me" in the manner of this very thoughtful gift.

I reached into the basket and pulled out a bottle of vanilla scented body spray, a tiny teddy bear wearing a blue and red sweater (Lillian had picked the bear out especially for me) and then I pulled out a small square jewelry box.

I opened the black velvet case and I began to cry; it was a locket. On the face of the locket was an angel sitting on a cloud looking down. I still wear this locket and each time I clasp the delicate chain around my neck I say a prayer for the family that bought this beautiful memento and the child that I gave life and so much love to.

Also, in the basket was a heart shaped clay container with a teddy bear on top. I took off the lid and peered inside. Engraved on the floor of the container was,

"I thank my God every time I remember you.

-Philippians 1:3."

To this day, this is still my favorite verse as it reminds me of my sweet Iris and her chosen family.

With tears in my eyes I once again thanked Lillian and her parents for their thoughtfulness and kindness.

Lillian peered at the sweet baby I had cradled in my arms. She said nothing, just staring at Iris.

"Would you like to hold her?" I asked as I looked to Annie for approval.

Annie smiled at me in support. I handed Iris to her and she took Iris to the hospital couch near my bed. Taking a seat, she waved Lillian over to her side and helped her skooch to the top of the seat.

My heart ached and exploded all at once. It seems contradictory for joy and sorrow to occur at the same time, but those two emotions sat perfectly side by side in my heart as I watched Annie and Lillian.

Bliss and grief seeped out my eyes and I patted the drops away with a tissue as I watched Annie tear up over her daughter meeting *our* daughter for the first time.

Annie kissed Lillian on the forehead and walked Iris back over to me. She placed Iris in my arms and touched my shoulder looking at me with tears in her eyes.

"We will be around if you want us, but we want to respect this time."

She caressed her thumb on my shoulder before she removed her hand and grasp Lillian's to walk out of the room.

That afternoon I then gave Iris her first bath, (which I got on video—I wanted to be able to look back on the special moments my daughter and I shared), I dressed her in a delicate white silk dress with small iridescent beads and pearly white embroidered vines. Many months prior I informed my church that I wanted to dedicate my baby to the Lord. So, my mother had bought her a beautiful white dress, which I put on her after her bath. It was marked newborn, but her tiny one-day old body was swimming in the gown.

One of my church's elders, Pastor Hank, came to my room to dedicate Iris. He brought with him a petite white Bible. To this day I still have this Bible, along with many pictures, video and keepsakes—which encompasses the contents of the basket Lillian brought me and the petite white dress Iris wore at this moment—in an elements-proof box in a safe place that I visit often.

Pastor Hank held Iris's tiny body as he prayed over her, asking the Lord to bless her life and calling upon the Lord to protect my heart. His prayers and many others were surely my lifeline in getting through this day and the ones to follow.

Why have her dedicated? I was not going to be her mother for much longer, right? Well, you are partially right, I am not her "*mommy*", I never will be—not that I did not long for that, but that is not my role in Iris's life. Sure, I spent months nauseated, throwing up and in total bodily discomfort, but I am not her mommy. I have stretch marks on my belly and scars on my loins and I have an aching in my heart to prove Iris is my child, but I am not her mommy. My title *does* have the profoundly unique and immensely great word, "mom". My heart and my soul love Iris so far and beyond, a love that only a mother could fully comprehend. My body shows that love that I had and still have for her, but I was not going to be her nurturer. Annie is the one who will mend her heart, kiss her boo-boos and be her safe place in times of trouble. Annie is the one who will be Iris's source of guidance and joy; Annie is Iris's mommy. I wanted to dedicate Iris because, like Annie, I would pray for her, which is one of the most powerful things a mother can do for her child and again, I am Iris's birth *MOM*. So, Pastor Hank came to help fulfill my desire to have her dedicated to the Lord.

Despite the coldness of the hospital room, it was a beautiful ceremony. Not a dry eye occupied that room, including Pastor Hank. It was cleansing for me to have this done; to be able to know in my heart and to announce in front of friends, family and God (Jeb, my parents and the Lovettes were there at this time) that this is my child and that I love her. And just because I will not physically, financially, and emotionally take

119

care of her, I will always hold her up in prayer—a promise I have kept through the years and will continue to uphold, especially present day, as I wrestle over reaching out to the Lovettes.

" *Only when we are brave enough to explore the darkness will we discover the infinite power of our light.*"

Brené Brown

Chapter 11

The Worst Day of My Life Part 2
January 15th, 2002

It was my last and final day in the hospital, more specifically, the last day with Iris had come. Helen, Annie, Lucas and I had planned for them to come at five o'clock for me to officially place Iris in the Lovette's arms. (Annie and Lucas very kindly, offered for me to come see Iris when she turned six months old, but I knew telling her good-bye once was going to be hard enough, my heart could not take doing it for a second time, so I declined, thus making this my final day with Iris.) As the day progressed and the hour hand got closer to five, I got more and more anxious. To be perfectly honest I could not wait for them to come. It was not that I did not want Iris, that was the farthest thing from the truth. It was that I sincerely could not bear holding her knowing I was to say goodbye in just a few short moments. I sat on the cold, vinyl covered hospital couch and cried, holding her close to my face, constantly kissing her forehead and her cheeks.

It was five o'clock, the Lovettes and Hellen were here. The plan was for us all to sit and talk and then around eight o'clock I would, as aforementioned, officially place my baby into the Lovette's arms.

I could not make it. After twenty minutes of holding Iris I softly whispered in her tiny ear, "I love you".

I squeezed her tight, trying to make my hug sink in to last a lifetime; tears that were already there became a river. I informed everyone that I did not wish to stay, that I *had* to go, not explaining that I was broken so badly inside, that I could not postpone this inevitable act any longer. My Father informed the nurse of my desire to leave and she brought a wheelchair into my room.

With quivering lips, I kissed Iris's velvet-soft forehead for the very last time and handed her over to Annie, her mommy. I, soaked in tears, bent over in emotional agony made my way to the wheelchair. Although, you would not have known by looking at me, I was trying to hold my emotions in. I was rolled down the hall, empty handed, put into the elevator and I went home.

I honestly do not remember the car ride home. Maybe it was a failed memory—I doubt this because I remember most everything else as if it was yesterday. Maybe I was in shock—but then why do I remember everything else? I believe the most likely reason is that the Lord took this memory from me. It was a memory of pain, but not a memory of learning, so the Lord wiped it clean to save me from carrying more hurt than my mind and soul could handle.

This I do remember, not just with my mind but with every fiber of my being; I walked into my childhood home, made my way up the first flight of stairs and wholly collapsed on the landing. My knees gave out under the weight of my grief. Frozen in place, lying in the fetal position I sobbed. In the pit of my belly there was an emptiness, not that there was a lack of child growing inside, but that there was no child, period. Depression had sunk in. I remember thinking,

> *"She is gone forever… she will never know the true depths of my love; she will never feel my hugs and kisses. I will never see her look into my eyes with such pure, sweet, unfiltered love again. I will never*

hold her, dry her tears, play with her, teach her."

The next morning, I, in my raw physical and emotional state, got up, dressed and headed to the courthouse with my Mother. I was to officially sign off on my parental rights to Iris. My authorization of the termination of my rights would give the adoption agency custodial custody of Iris until six months after I sign this pending documentation, when the Lovette family would finalize the adoption of Iris taking sole, legal custody of her.

I stepped into the Judge's large, cherrywood paneled room with my mother. Helen was already in the room waiting for me. As always, she was well dressed and eager to support me in *whatever* I chose.

"Hi Jenn, are you doing okay" Helen asked empathetically while taking up my hand into hers.

"Hi Helen," I said with a half-smile. "Thank you so much for all you have done to help me through this adoption process. I am so glad Iris is going to live with Lucas and Annie. I know this is for the best."

Helen turned to my mother and greeted her with the same empathy and kindness she had shown me.

We went to sit down in the red leather chairs in front of a large mirror-polished, cherrywood desk to wait for the Judge to come in. My heart was racing, my stomach in a knot, but I was clear of my mind, knowing that this coming heart ache was to give Iris a Dad, to give her stability and healthy emotional, financial and mental support. This was what I saw to be the greatest good for my child, so as her mother I knew this sacrifice was best.

"The Judge will be in shortly to officiate the relinquishment of your parental rights. Not only will you be signing papers, but you will also have to verbalize your relinquishment, because all of this will be recorded to be kept on file."

I nodded in understanding.

Helen smiled warmly at me.

"When the judge comes in and asks you questions make sure you verbalize a yes or a no so that it is on the recorder. Unfortunately, technology has not come far enough to pick up the sound of a head nod."

I cracked a smile at her joke, and she squeeze my hand with a quick tight squeeze before she let it go.

"You would think this courthouse would have some tissues available!"

Helen said while searching the room. She knew me from our few visits, I am a crier, and would surely need a tissue for this occasion. Helen found a box just outside the court room on the credenza in the hall. She set it on the small, cherry end table between my mother and me.

Helen placed her hand on my shoulder after she set the tissues beside me. With a warm smile Helen looked me in the eyes and asked,

"Are you sure this is what you want? Because if not I can make this all go away. Whatever you want is what will happen. But I want to remind you that once these papers are signed your parental rights are permanently surrendered."

I grabbed a tissue from the box beside me and wiped away the tears that were welling in my eyes.

"I am sure." More words danced in my head about how I wanted to parent Iris so badly, but how I knew Lucas was a precious, irreplaceable gift to my daughter that I did not want her to miss out on, but those thoughts never left my lips, but escaped in more tears running down my face.

The dark cherrywood walls and furniture, muted red leather chairs and all-around detachment from warmth in the room was a bit intimidating. I was about to sign off on my parental rights, something so personal, profound and loving, yet it was being done in this comfort-void, once tissue lacking room in front of a Judge as if I had committed a crime and I was to be unempathetically sentenced. But, no matter the atmosphere, I knew what had to be done. At this point, I was the only one who had the power to get up, walk out, head back to the hospital and take Iris back to my parent's house for a life of struggle with an earthly father who would bring her heartache and hopelessness, or I could sign the covenant and give Iris more, give her a loving earthly father who, prayerfully, would bring her joy and hope, and a life filled with more possibilities.

My love for her trumped my desire to parent her, my intimidation of that room and the sorrow within me. I was only seventeen, but my love for this tiny, helpless child was that of a mother, not that of a self-indulgent teen. Though the room was lacking comfort, the Lord gave me strength, courage and steadfast mind to see that signing these papers is hands down the greater option for Iris to flourish.

With my mind set on the goal of making Iris Lovette my daughter's official name, the man to oversee my choice and record my voice comes walking from a side door hidden in the cherry paneling.

He was wearing his official black robe with a light blue color and red tie breaming from the neck. I'm not sure if it was the coldness of the room or the officiality of the Judges dress, but I felt a bit dehumanized in that space. Like I was a case number, a mere appointment in this court's schedule, and not a hurting human in need of hospitality, empathy or warmth.

"Jennifer Mae." The judge stated through his sober demeanor.

"Yes, I am Jennifer Mae." I responded, trying to mirror his soberness to help fight off the tears that were building up in my eyes again.

"I am Judge Perflin, and it is my understanding you are here in my court house today, Janurary 16th of the year 2002, to sign off a termination of your parental rights to the girl child born to you, Jennifer Mae, on Janurary 12th at 8:04pm at St. Mary's hospital in Deep Valley, Pennsylvania.

"Thha-a-t is correct." At this point my tears where no longer contained and my voice had started to quack through the weight of my grief.

Over recording, the Judge asked me if I was here on my own free will, if I understood what I was doing and the finality of this choice. All to which, through copious weeping, I said, "Yes."

The judge then asked me to state why I was placing my child for adoption, to which, again, I sobbed through my answer,

"Because I cannot provide for my daughter as I believe she deserves."

My true answer to this question could have been a novel's worth of words, but my emotions kept my reply short and bittersweet.

I then placed the black ink pen to the relinquishment documentation and painted my love for my child in the form of my signature next to the X; thereby, officially, gaining my title, "birth mom", and losing my legal ability to parent Iris.

Before this moment I was a biological mom. I had intent to place my child, but that intent did not acquire my present title. Being called a, "birth mom" previous to me signing the necessary documents to surrender my parental rights would have been potentially coercive to my self-determination of choosing my own parenting plan; a possible self-fulfilling prophecy that no agency, adoptive parents nor biological parent should desire to chance.

By gaining my title, Iris was kept from a life of despair and struggle with me, and obtained a different, prayerfully better life with the Lovettes. I gained a life without Jeri in and out to drain and belittle me. I gave so much through this process, but I *never* once "gave up".

A mother has an inborn yearning to protect her children at all cost and that is exactly what I did—I protected my child, the best I could, from what I viewed as a life of hurt, struggle and reoccurring loss and gave her the safety I lacked in my environment and my current being.

Helen got up from her seat, quickly thanked the Judge for his time, then walked over to me and held me as my body shook from my weeping. Once she pulled back, she tugged another tissue from its box, placed it in my palm and clasped my fingers around it.

Helen then took my mother's and my hand in hers and squeezed them gently as she said, "You have done an amazingly selfless and loving thing for Iris. Now here is where you need to give yourself grace and time to grieve and then you, yourself need to flourish. Build a life that Iris would be proud of."

I smiled through my slowing tears and responded to Helen with all I could muster after such an emotional tax to my system, "I will."

Helen let go of our hands and hugged my mother and I one last time. She reminded us of the pictures and letters that were to come of Iris and her family. Then my mother and I set out to head back home to begin the grieving process...

So many days and nights I longed for Iris, crying with little pause. My father sweetly gave up his place in bed to allow me to sleep with my mother, so that I was never alone.

The pain was not only in my heart, mind and soul; it was also in my body. During labor, as I previously mentioned, I tore despite getting an episiotomy—a fourth degree tear. The healing process was difficult, to say the least. Sitting down was a chore in having to sit on an air-filled plastic ring to elevate my stitches from coming in contact with the seat. Hot baths were my body's only comfort and the burn from the initial dunk was horrendous, and even in the bath, the air-filled donut followed me. My exterior muscles ached for a few weeks after, but the blood pumping muscle behind my ribs ached for many years.

Placing my daughter for adoption was *the* hardest thing I had ever gone through, and I am sure will ever go through. Yet, I know in my heart it was the best thing I could have done given my circumstances, first and foremost for Iris, second for me.

Had I chosen to parent Iris, she would have had all the love a mother has to give, but she would not receive the attention she deserved, considering I would have had to work many hours to support her needs and attend high school. Along with my time away I would have likely fallen deeper into the need for egocentric reassurance. Being a mother can be a lonely undertaking; I can only imagine I would have felt that isolation tenfold being a mom when the rest of my cohorts were being kids. Furthermore, Iris would not have had a loving father in her life had her biological father chosen to also be absent from her life outside the womb; from what I understood, she probably would have been worse off had Jeri chosen to occasionally pop in.

I signed the legal papers to protect Iris, not because I was ambivalent towards my love of her. My love went deep enough to break my own heart for what I saw as her well-being.

" Grief is not a disorder, a disease or a sign of weakness. It is an emotional, physical and spiritual necessity, the price you pay for love. The only cure for grief is to grieve."

Earl A. Grollman

Chapter 12

Postpartum and Situational Depression
2002-2004

For those of you who have never experienced depression I am going to try to explain it to you in a comprehensible way. Not because I want you to really feel my pain, I would never wish that kind of pain on anyone, but perhaps this can help you *empathize* with someone suffering from this type of mental illness and therein give them your loving ears to listen and two compassionate arms to hug them.

Do you remember as a child being so bored because there is quite literally (in your mind) nothing to do; the feeling of utter despair that you just have to sit inside and do nothing all day. *Longing for something, but not being able to quench that thirst.*

Do you remember your stomach being in knots over the unknown? The knot in your belly right before you ask your crush to the dance, tell your mom you broke her favorite knick-knack or trying out for a school play or a promotion at work. *The feelings of being so anxious and so aware of your short comings.*

Now, add the feeling of your crush saying no, your mom over-reacting in an entirely negative way and totally bombing your audition or interview. *Lost, lonely, unworthy, despair, anxious, failure.*

Those feelings combined is the closest description that I can give unto how I felt every waking moment for the first two years after Iris's birth.

Please, do not miss-read my condition. I knew in my heart that I made the best choice for Iris and for myself, but I am her mother; for nine months I carried that sweet girl, I agonized through the pains of pregnancy and delivery for her because I loved her—and I still love her. Because of this great love, I was grieving over my loss of her and my loss of being a mommy.

I believe that God allowed me to go through teenage pregnancy and the loss of my child so that I could gain my own life. He knew that nothing short of me going through this experience would save me. I was not a safe or healthy person previous to finding out I was pregnant. I was self-absorbed and desperately seeking the approval of man. Placing my daughter's needs over my own was the only thing that was going to change my heart and get me back on the right path to be the woman God has called me to be.

In my progress to the right path, depression medication, or "happy pills" as I called them, were an essential part of my every step. I also saw a Christian psychiatrist for two and a half years after Iris's birth, which having Dr. Renee was vital to me processing my grief.

I felt like everyone was moving on and expecting me to do the same. Talking with Dr. Renee about how I was feeling, even years after the placement, was essential to my healing. I felt as though those around me did not fully grasp what I was going through and consequently expected me to have a timeline to my grief, but I was stuck in it. I felt that I had to keep these deep, hard to deal with emotions to myself because others did not want to hear them, yet again. But Dr. Renee gave me her loving ear and she helped to validate my grief and work through it at my own, healthy pace without judgment or pressure to meet a time quota.

We are given a divine example in the New Testament of not holding our emotions in, an example of speaking our grief and moving forward with it. Jesus willingly died on the cross, He longed to be with us for eternity, but do you know what Jesus did before He willingly bore our sins on the cross? He dropped to His knees, He wept, and He prayed. Jesus was scared, overwhelmed and sad to the point of sweating blood, yet, despite *choosing* the greatest good—God's will—He did not withhold His emotions, He laid them at His Father's feet.

Who am I to hold these emotions in when Jesus has so clearly shown that even though we choose something does not mean that we are not allowed to feel emotions that may show that we are scared, sad and overwhelmed with what we chose?

I have learned through Dr. Renee and Jesus that what I feel is valid; I am allowed to express my feelings in a healthy manner so that I can work through them. It does NOT matter what I think others think I should be feeling (e.g. putting a timeline to my grief, or, I *chose* placement, so I don't have the right to grieve, and other harmful thoughts and opinions I thought others held about me). What matters is that I work through my valid emotions and grief in my unique, but earnest loss in a healthy style. Also, that I have the understanding that, yes, my feelings are valid, but they are not my master; I am the master of my feelings.

The example of Jesus and speaking with Dr. Renee was a huge help, but I still desperately missed Iris; I was still in the thick of depression. I was grieving hard, but my grief does not equate regret. My grief was instituted in the loss of my child and the bottomless love that I have for her, and the sorrow I had from past hurt and present abandonment. But I do not regret giving Iris a different life than the one she would have had with me.

It was not until God placed Andrew in my life when the depression let loose of its life-sucking hold on me and I began to be genuinely happy again. That is not to say that all women who place their child for adoption find healing through a man. This is my unique journey. God used Andrew to restore my effervescence. I was emotionally shattered and so hurt from my relationship with my own father which is why I sought validation from a man in the worldly sense in the first place. God loved me so much that He saw me, and He acknowledged me in my aching.

Because of my cries of heartache, and God's love for me He was moved to send Andrew to me to show me that I am worthy of love, a valuable, likable woman with so much more to offer than my sexuality. I needed my original brokenness, lingering from my childhood, to be mended so that I could see my worth, see that life is so much more than running after meaningless, unfulfilling validation in the flesh.

Seek a man that doesn't ask you to prove your love. Seek a man that will prove God's love."

Shannon L. Alder

Chapter 13

The Man Who Helped to Make Me Whole

2004-always and forever

He had always been there. Andrew was the six foot nine, shy boy walking the high school halls. He was two grades ahead of me and other than acknowledging his height, I never gave him a second thought. But he had noticed me I am sure; there are not very many girls who waddled the halls of high school, pregnant at sixteen to seventeen years old.

In high school, I was fortunate enough that throughout my pregnancy I was never teased, degraded, nor *publicly* looked down upon. My classmates were not understanding of my situation, but they were kind. I am so thankful that they did not treat me like I was unworthy and ruined. I suppose though I was degraded at one point in my pregnancy, that is, if you account for the phone call my father received. You see, the biological father, Jeri, had told his parents that I was pregnant. So, Jeri's father called my father to inform him that I was a, and I quote, "Slut."

Of course, my father stood up for me, but I was still hurt by that man's words, although they were not directly said to me, and truthfully, to this day I do not know why my father told me the exact words that Jeri's father had used. I could have gone without hearing someone call me a slut in such a raw time, even if it was second hand.

Today I know I am a daughter of God, that my worth is in Jesus Christ, not in anyone's demeaning, or praising words for that matter, but at the time I was not so aware of that, especially since I was feeling like the worst daughter Christ or my earthly father had ever had.

Here I am, wandering aloud through my thoughts again. Let's get back to the focus of this chapter.

It was not until Andrew graduated from high school that I gave him the second thought, the third thought...Many of my evenings were spend at a joint friend's house watching the boys play video games. (I loved to watch people play video games. I grew up in the 90's with an older brother, "You can have a turn when I die." My brother would dictate. But, being four years younger than my brother, I spent most of my time watching him play Nintendo with a few seconds of play for myself before I quickly died in between.) If we were not over at a friend's house, we were out bowling or playing pool at the local pool house.

I so relished in Andrew's hilarious personality and how he respected my boundaries. He was the total opposite of Jeri. He valued that I enjoyed the company of friends and never tried to stop me from having close friendships with other people. He also honored my loss. He could handle my tough days and never once made me feel like I could not speak of Iris or be on the outside what I felt like on the inside. Andrew was a safe person.

At school, I found myself getting butterflies sitting at my desk during my last period of the day. The butterflies would go crazy when the clock hit 2:20pm; it would mean only a few minutes before I got out of school and would go straight to his house. He was alluring; from the way he smelled like fireplace, apples and man, to the way he made me smile, continuously and whole heartedly, something that had not been on my face, and more importantly in my heart for a very long time.

On one of my afterschool visits we were watching a movie. Which movie it was, I do not remember because I was working on building up the courage to ask him something that would leave me very vulnerable had he said no.

"Can I kiss you?" I asked looking at him with a sincere, but small smile.

I remember dreaming as a child how absolutely fantastic it would be to be asked that question by a boy. That day never came, so, just as I am today, if I am not going to be romanced the way I want, I am going to romance another so that I can still experience the thrill. Knowing that Andrew was extremely shy when it came to stepping out of his comfort zone or asking difficult questions, I believed if I did not speak up that our friendship would not have gone beyond movies, pool, mutual friends and video games. Being that he made me feel safe and valued I wanted to be more than *just* one of his friends.

He looked at me puzzled and I panicked. What had I done? Here I had this wonderful friendship going with this amazing, Christian man who made me so, so happy and I have ruined it

148

with being too forward. Before I had the time to react to his reaction (other than my cheeks flushing and my mind going a million miles a second) he, uncharacteristically walked closer to me. Andrew grabbed my hand and with his other hand he swiped his thumb across my flushed cheek, pushing a brown curl out of my face.

He bent down to meet my much shorter stance and kissed me softly for a respectable length of time and pulled back to look me in my eyes and gave me such a handsome, earnest smile.

His kiss was a sweet, romantic kiss. A kiss that was full of passion, but not sex; with love, but not lust.

For a while, despite knowing him quite well, I felt as though I was kissing a stranger, though we were dating (unofficially) for months. I often could only picture the tall awkward boy walking past me in the hall, never making eye contact. The boy I only saw but did not "see". This feeling eventually dissipated and what was left in place of the novelty was complete security. Andrew had this over whelming sense of peace about him. The same peace that I felt sitting next to the Christmas tree showed up again in this very sweet man. The same peace that only a real, present and interested God can give.

God has a mysterious and amazing way of making things come together for His redeeming purpose in our lives. God used me to help heal Andrew's brokenness, just as much as He used Andrew for my healing.

Andrew came from a home with a mother who worked extremely hard to provide for him and his sister and part of that was to save each penny that she brought in. To save money, Andrew's mother never bought name brand clothes, something that was not important to Andrew to have, but the children in his elementary and middle school relentlessness teased him for not having logoed clothes and another source of their teasing was his height. Andrew was much taller than his classmates even in his tiny youth.

Andrew was presently shy because he had learned to keep to himself. When he did not let people in, he would not risk being hurt, like he had been by so many people before. I was the opposite in being extremely extroverted. I wanted to let people in, so I could find acceptance through relationships. Between our two personalities, our two coping mechanisms if you will, we managed to make each other grow in our own self-esteem and comfort of being who we are God created to be. He taught me to slow down, to think before I act and to be more fruitful in self-control of who I choose to be in my life. I had thought my whole life that relationships are what will fulfil me, and while God did create me to be a relational person, I was putting all my eggs into that single basket, not being choosey about who I let close.

Sure, Jesus was kind and caring to the actively sinning, He did spend time with them to reach their lost souls and so should I, but Jesus was also choosey in who He let get close, not spending all His time while He was on earth with those who were lost. He had the twelve disciples that were like-minded men, following God's teaching. Jesus had an even closer relationship with three of the disciples, Peter, James and John. These three men were like iron sharpening Jesus. He allowed these men to have a deep relationship with Him because they were good influences, refined Him and held Him accountable. Andrew helped me see that I needed to be more intentional, like Jesus, with my relational life.

I, on the other hand, unintentionally taught Andrew to open to others, as not everyone is looking to hurt him. But I did intentionally teach him to stand his ground when he was hurt. His past had left him so passive, so unconfrontational that when hurt would happen to him, he would shut down. Not that I taught him to lash back, but to speak his truth, to see that he is worth having the kindness and respect of others.

God taught us through each other that we are likeable, worthy people and no amount of hurt in our past, present or future could abstain our worth because our value is in the one who fearfully and wonderfully created us, the one who died for us and defeated that death three days later. We learned that love and security means supporting each other through the hard emotions and difficult seasons of our lives. Though I was not aware at this time how much I helped Andrew because I was so consumed with my own grief that I could not fully comprehend his, I did notice that he came more alive as I was also thriving, moving out of my constant sorrow.

I had had my fair share of boyfriends in the past, none which made me feel the way Andrew did. He was a gentleman who treated me like a lady. He would go out of his way to ensure I was comfortable; he took care of me emotionally, which I was not used to from the men in my life. He would get me a blanket if he saw I was cold—he noticed me—wrap it around me, tuck me in and kiss the top of my head. What really melted me was that he always opened the car door for me—which I would always promptly thank him for with a kiss on the cheek. I have had boys open doors for me, that was nice, but to have a car door opened for me was like the ultimate gesture to make me feel like a real lady, like I was loved, cherished and adored.

Andrew and I, one evening, had just arrived at my home after dinner and a movie. He walked around to my car door, opened it and grasped my hand to gently pull me up. We went inside my home, I sat on the couch in my family room and turned on the television. Andrew noticed me. He saw that I was a bit chilly and grabbed me a blanket from the rack and tucked me in and around midnight he left to go back to his home.

The next morning, I awoke to get my usual cup of coffee.

"Jenn," My father pulled for my attention.

"Yeah, Dad?" I said, waiting for him to communicate something negative about Andrew being over so late.

"If a boy really loves you, he would be willing to anything within reason for you."

I was a little taken aback that he did not mention that I cannot have company over so late, or the type of company—a male—I had, but I believe he was right.

Andrew fit that benchmark above and beyond. I believe my father saw how much of a positive influence Andrew was on my life and my healing. He saw how Andrew was bringing out this vibrancy in me that he had never known before. More than just my earthly father's criteria for a man worth marrying, Andrew fit God's check list of a forever and always love:

> *"Love is patient, love is kind. It does not envy, it does not boast, it is not proud. It does not dishonor others, it is not self-seeking, it is not easily angered, it keeps no record of wrongs. Love does not delight in evil but rejoices with the truth. It always protects, always trusts, always hopes, always perseveres."*
>
> *-1 Corinthians 13:4-7*

"Love is patient"; Andrew did not hurry me; he did not make me feel like I had a timeline to my grief. Rather he took my hand and walked along with me, at my pace, down my hard path to healing.

"Love is kind"; Andrew was and is, earnestly, the kindest man I have ever had the pleasure of knowing. He treated me with such tender care, making me a priority. He showed me what kindness from a man looks like.

"Love does not envy"; Andrew knew of my placement and my depression. He did not make me feel as though he was unable to handle my grief, or that he wished I was like other girls without so much heavy hurt. He made me feel special, not because of my unique circumstances, but because of the irreplaceable person he viewed me as.

"Love does not boast"; Andrew never once held it over my head that he is a great man for being there for me in my time of need. He, at no time, talked of his goodness with pride, but was simply there for me without seeking verbal—or physical—thanks.

"Love is not proud"; Andrew was humble, not only in his words, but in the way he carried himself.

"Love does not dishonor others"; Andrew was so respectful of my parents, and beyond that he chose to spend time with them—he enjoyed their company.

"Love is not self-seeking"; Andrew would treat me kindly. He would speak words of affirmation unto me and he would gift me with his time and with the occasional sweet note or gift. He did this all, not to get something from me, but purely to make my heart smile.

"Love is not easily angered"; Andrew was shy, consequently he was slow to speak, but he was also slow to anger. He was a passionate man, but his passions did not cause rage.

"Love keeps no record of wrongs"; Andrew never once used manipulation, nor did he make me feel beneath him for walking in the shoes of a birth mom. He praised me for my hard decision to give Iris a different life and reminded me often that I am a strong and amazing woman, deeply loved by my creator and by him.

"Love does not delight in evil but rejoices in truth"; I grew up thinking I was not liked by my father, then I was abandoned by the man who fathered my child. The devil was delighted to really hit those facts hard into my heart; he was more than happy to slither those lies into my mind and persuade me that all men have no desire to value me. Andrew was swift to assure me that I am not ruined, unworthy nor am I unlikeable. Not only did his words reassure me that I am valuable, not only to the Heavenly Father who fearfully and wonderfully created me, but I am of great value to him.

"Love always protects"; Andrew was happy to hear my true emotions and I felt safe to share them with him. He was not annoyed in hearing my truth over and over; he was glad that

I felt amply safe and stable in our relationship to share my true emotions as often as I needed.

"Love always trusts"; Andrew valued my words and took them as truth. He listens whole heartedly; he did not just wait his turn to speak.

"*Love always hopes*"; When I felt hopeless, lost in grief, Andrew was always there to bring me back to the place of hope. He reminded me that God cares for me enough to send Andrew to walk with me along my hard path to healing and happiness. He also repeated to me that I will always walk in the shoes of a birth mom, but the path those shoes walk will not always be this hard, nor are my chosen footwear my identity—my brave, strong, loving attributes given to me by the one who fearfully and wonderfully created me spoke more to my character than any garment I have or ever could put on.

"*Love always perseveres*"; I would often cry to Andrew telling him how I felt ruined and broken, that I was worried that he would leave me, as Jeri did. I was emotionally broken, and in this state, I was shown previously through Jeri that men do not stick around on the hard path, but Andrew was eager to show me my reference was wrong; love stays, no matter how hard it gets.

I was captivated by Andrew, not just by him as a handsome member of the opposite sex, but by how me made me feel; lovable, likable and beautiful, not just on the outside. He was a man of God, a 1 Corinthians man, and I so effortlessly fell for him because of that. God knew Andrew was exactly what my heart needed to heal from my past and to have find joy.

But he was not going to be mine for much longer. Andrew's parents had had their house for sale for four years prior and, of course, it finally sold a few months into our newly orientated relationship. He was going to move, and it would be all over.

However, distance did not dull our passion or our love for each other as I feared it would. We would talk on the phone every night for hours on end, never running out of things to say. We never had the awkward silence some couple would have on the phone, the silence that clearly says, "hang up," but they never do. Talking came so easy to us.

Andrew and I often talk about how God made his parents wait four long years to sell their home. Four long years so that I could find my husband and Andrew could find his wife. Things really do happen for a reason—for the greater good of those who believe in God.

May 30th of 2004 Andrew, over the long distance of the telephone, officially asked me to be his—first and only—girlfriend. Although if you were to ask Andrew about his dating record he would smugly confess with a big, dumb smile on his face that I was not his first girlfriend. He claims in the third grade he had a romantic relationship with two of his fellow classmates, a.k.a. they held hands.

"Third and Fourth grade, because I was a Mack Daddy." He would always correct me to insure I knew of his "allure over the ladies"—he has always been able to make me laugh.

We dated long distance, and it was the most thrilling, love lusting experience of my life. Do not get me wrong, it was awful not seeing him whenever I wanted, but it was like wanting ice cream. When you have not had it in a while, you craved it in the pit of your belly, your taste buds longed for it, and when you finally do have it again, it is sweeter and more satisfying because of the wait.

We would talk on the phone every night for hours at a time, but even at that, it was not enough. We needed more of each other. At least once a month one of us would take the one way five-hundred-mile drive to see the other. When it was my turn to take the drive, I would pack my little blue car, print out my directions from Deep Valley, Pennsylvania to Sevierville, Tennessee and I would head out.

The adrenalin rush and the radio blaring made the seven-hour drive seem like a breeze, until I would reach Knoxville, Tennessee. At that point I would be forty-five minutes away from seeing him. The adrenalin rush would turn into butterflies and I became like an anxious five-year-old, not capable of understanding time.

"FOURTH OF JULY SUPERMARKET Exit 407".

I would see the first billboard for this glorious place and the wings of the butterflies in my belly would work into a dancing, twirling frenzy. Andrew always met me here, not that the place was significant to us, but that it was effortlessly seen because of the bright, sparkly red and blue print on the front of the building, and it was right off the exit. He started meeting me here because the route to his parents' house from this point forward was down country back roads and he was not sure the first few times I visited that I would be able to find my way. Once I was familiar with the area, we still met at the Fourth of July Supermarket, and at that point this place became significant, *our* meeting spot.

After nine months' worth of phone calls, traveling and ice cream Andrew finally decided he could not take it anymore; he had to be near me. He packed up his white Dodge Stratus and made the final trip to Pennsylvania from Tennessee.

My parents are conservative; my father is a pastor's child and thus he reflected the strict values and stuck to the tight rules of his upbringing. No boys in the bedroom, no boys sleeping over; even if they are in another room. Heck, I even remember one time as a kid, my father came into my Grandmother's family room where all my cousins and I were laying down on separate air mattresses in preparation for sleep— aka giggling—and he split us all up; girls went to one room and boys went to another. Even *cousins* of the opposite sex could not sleep in the same room. Perhaps my dad lived in a different era where cousins commonly took to each other? Who knows, that is just an example of how averse my dad is to boys sleeping over. So, when my dad allowed Andrew to set up a bed *and* have a dresser in our basement—dresser designates the objective of an extended stay—it was a real shocker. But again, my Father knew that Andrew was a good man and he wanted him to stay a part of my life. My dad even started to tease Andrew and I that he did not like him because with boyfriends in the past that he had communicated that he did not like I would run to them even more. My father wanted Andrew to stick around.

Two weeks in Andrew had a job and had found a place to live—outside my parent's house—and two roommates to live with. He was officially a permanent fixture in my life. We dated for two glorious years and one more year of me asking him when he is going to "pop the question". If you were to ask me—or any other woman in my situation—I was not over-the-top whiney about getting a ring on my finger but, Andrew may have another rendition to the story (are you reading the eye rolls in between my words ha-ha).

I did not want to marry Andrew so badly because I wanted to have his child. That is not even remotely close to what I was thinking. I wanted to marry him because I wanted to have slumber parties with him; to be able to stay up late enjoying his company and then to wake up the next morning with him by my side. I loved him so much that seeing him during the day and saying our good-byes at night was not enough. I longed to be with him, and he longed to be with me. We were in love and that was the only motivation in our marriage—to be with and to love each other.

Andrew did not make me forget Iris, no one could do that. What he did do was help me to fill my cup with positive self-esteem, joy and other attributes God had always desired for me and he satisfied the need to be loved and accepted by a safe man. Andrew understood that his fulfillment of that need was precious. He knew it was not to fulfill me sexually—with momentary bliss—but to fill me the way God had intended my cup to overflow.

God used Andrew to help heal my derivation wound and open my eyes and heart to how a big God could possibly love me, care about me and desire a relationship with me. Andrew was not the cultural lie of a perfect puzzle piece man that finally fit my missing half to make me whole. Andrew was the beautiful instrument that God used to help me heal and become full in Christ. God is my redeemer and the savior of my soul, not any man, not even Andrew has that power over me for it was Christ at work through him.

Becoming requires an uneasiness in the being, but beauty is not deviant from the pain of growth.

Chapter 14

Butterflies; A Benign Symbol Turned Profound

May 2007-May 2008

Growing up I loved the outdoors. Fishing, hiking, camping, and playing in the mucky water of the pond in my back yard searching for water bugs and tad poles to scoop up with my five-gallon white bucket. But as far as loving a single animal over all the rest, it just was not something I thought about. Do not get me wrong I thought butterflies and tadpoles were neat, but I did not have posters of them plastering my childhood bedroom walls. Sure, I did have unicorns standing in sun beams surrounded by rays of rainbows, but as far as real animals go, I did not fancy one more over the other.

May 19th, the eve of our three-year anniversary. We went to Hocking Hills, Ohio to celebrate our love, and quite honestly, I knew, well, I hoped so hard that I could have sworn I knew, that Andrew would finally ask me to be his wife. We got to our camp site, pitched our purple and green three-room tent—necessary space for the two of us—and went to Cedar Falls. While on the path to the beautiful waterfall, we encountered a small pool of water. Butterflies flew all around us and covered the pebble-laced ground. I was in awe of not just the multitude of these tiny creatures but the overwhelming beauty of the whole scene.

"I can't wait any longer" I heard Andrew say from behind me.

I was bending over trying to get one of the orange beauties to climb onto my hand. I thought nothing of his statement, so I tried for a few more seconds to get a butterfly to cooperate with me. No such luck, so I turned around to see what Andrew was talking about.

Down on one knee with a blue velvet box containing the loveliest ring I had ever laid eyes upon; marquee center stone, two round stones snuggling the center marquee and crisscrossing bands of tiny diamonds on either side glimmered in the ray of lights beaming through the canopy of leaves.

"I love you so much Jenn. Will you marry me?" Andrew's voice quaked.

"Of course!" I said with zero delay between his words and mine.

Excited and full of adrenaline, we attempted to continue down the path to view Cedar Falls, but we were just too excited to "merely" look at nature. We had to go back to our camp site and tell the whole world what had just happened.

Fast forward one year and a whole lot of planning later, I was walking down the aisle to marry my Andrew, my safe person, my best friend. Decorations of rainbows and unicorns were not to be found, despite how disappointed my eight-year-old self would have been. But what every table had was at least one tiny realistic looking butterfly perched on a clear glass vase of persimmon, yellow, terracotta and orange flowers. The butterfly; a symbol of beauty and change morphing from egg to larva, larva to caterpillar, caterpillar to cocoon and finally from cocoon to a beautiful butterfly. I too was going through a beautiful, but hard change. I was morphing with each step of aching growth, into the woman God has called me to be. I had been this tiny egg of a girl, just a shell of who God intended me to be. I grew to be a worm searching for my fulfillment, never finding my peace nor my place. Then Andrew came into my life through God's purpose and plan; he helped to wrap me in a safe, healthy space where I felt belonging and love so that I could have the strength and courage to grow from all the pain and mature from the lessons I had gorged myself on.

The butterfly that meant nothing to me previously is now a significant symbol of how God allowed me to go through stages of crawling around in my own strength and will, devouring worldly, fleeting pleasures. I had to go through the ugly and hard stage in order to be broken enough to let God in, so I would be ready and able to receive His peace, hope and safety. Without the pain of my own misguided comfort seeking I never would have found my way to Christ, nor would I have learned to unlock the beauty He had always intended me to bestow.

"All my longings lie open before you, Lord;
my sighing is not hidden from you."

Psalm 38:9

Chapter 15

Wanting It More Than Most Knew

2008

"We're not going to have children until we are financially stable and own our own home, even if that means we aren't having kids until we're forty."

I wanted children desperately, so hearing Andrew say that to me after six months of marriage was heart-breaking and quite frankly, devastating.

By no means was it that money was of no concern to me, or that we were poor—we were lower middle class, but middle class, nonetheless. I placed Iris for adoption because I was not financially capable of caring for her—along with other reasons previously stated—so yes, money was important, but the gut-wrenching terror that I was being forced to wait until I was forty to try for a child, and it may be too biologically late, was a huge burden on my heart. I struggled with the notion of not being able to conceive. That Iris was my one and only chance for a biological child, and that chance is now gone.

Andrew held strong to his belief that an abundance of money and owning our own home, rather than just renting is the utmost importance, and neither time nor rationalizing on my behalf could change his mind.

I do not think I fully grasp his reasoning at the time. I grew up in a home with a father who amply provided for our financial needs. I had never gone without any material objects I needed, but Andrew knew the struggle of poverty and did not want to go into fatherhood without having an overabundance of finances. I understood the need to have financial security, but I did not fully grasp the feeling and the fear that came with poverty.

172

May 14th, 2008, almost a year after marrying my best friend and six months into waiting on my husband to feel at ease with having a child, Andrew held his nephew—then two weeks and three days old—for the very first time. His heart was softened. He wanted a child of his own and I wanted to shout praises of joy to the Lord because I did not have to wait until it was potentially too late to try for a child.

It had always been my childhood dream to have kids before I turned twenty-five; I was now twenty-three (almost twenty-four). My reasoning was so that I could be a younger Grandma so that I could enjoy my grandbabies. I am not really sure if little girls normally think this way, but children were a staple in my life back then—my mother ran a day care out of her home—so I planned my life around children being a staple in adulthood too. I was so excited to see my childhood dream coming true.

I did my research, and lot of it, as I was determined to have a child. I knew it took women under thirty, on average, three months to conceive, but not to call a doctor until a year of trying had lapsed without conceiving. After the first month of trying I was overwhelmed with sadness that I had not become pregnant; the thoughts of, what if Iris was my one and only chance filled my head and prayers filled my heart. I get that most would think that one month of trying should not make a woman sad because so many women go through years of rollercoaster emotions trying to conceive. The two weeks wait after ovulation, the excitement of the potential positive pregnancy test and then the total let down of the negative strip seeming to mock your empty womb. But, as in all people, I had a back story to my sorrow. I had longed for a child for years prior to taking this test. Years ago, I had had one positive that resulted in a child, but not parenthood and this was finally my chance to claim a child of my own and it felt like parenthood was slipping through my fingers like water through a fragmented pail. I felt broken. I finally wanted to get pregnant and it was not as easy as my teenage body would have had me think. I grieved my lost chance at parenthood and did my best to not think about my next chance to arise.

Come the second month I was devastated when the stick read not pregnant. I so desperately wanted a child that a little, "bump in the road", got me into a panic. I badly wanted to be with child on July 23rd, 2008. That was the day Andrew and I were baptized. How perfect that would have been to announce to the world that I am starting a new life, not just within my soul, but within my womb. But that was not what God had planned for us. I believe God wanted my spiritual health to be well cared for before Andrew and I brought another person into our lives, so God made us wait and find rest in Him during the time of waiting.

Waiting is definitely not my strong suit, so I had quite a bit of growing in that area during this time. And even though I was being taught the hard lesson of waiting on God, I could never wait until my missed period, so I used the test that shows you six days before. Without fail—I was watching my cycle like a hawk—six days before I was to start, I would take the test. I was in the bathroom of our apartment at Mountain View Shores when I took my third month's test. I nervously waited and prayed, "Lord, please. Please, Lord, please." As I tried to keep my butterflies from spilling out my belly. Once the timer went off, I picked up the stick, squeezed my eyes tight and prayed one last time, "Lord, if it's your will, please let me be pregnant, please. And if not, Lord give me peace."

My knees gave out; I dropped to the floor and sobbed. A whispered, "Thank you." Were the only words I was able to release. I was pregnant. *I was a mommy*. I am not really sure how long I spent on that floor, but I finally calmed my sobs and turned them into songs of praise.

My Heavenly Father had heard the desires of my heart and granted them to me. Euphorically joyous is how I would describe my emotions at that time—I remember the feeling vividly, as if it was yesterday. Pure excitement and relief; this child would be and is so loved. This child was mine. I was finally getting my chance to be a mommy.

Now, before I give off the wrong impression, I want this to be understood—this child was not born out of the purpose of replacement for my last. This child is loved and wanted because she is her own person, because I wanted to be a mommy and because my husband and I love each other so much that we wanted to share our love with another, not because I needed to fill a void. Yes, I had a void for years after Iris's birth, but that hole was healed. God sent me Andrew, not to fill the hole in my heart, but to help me work to nurse it back to health.

Andrew was at work when I took my test, but I just could not wait for him to come home that night to tell him. So, I gather a card and an envelope wrote down, "I love you so much, 'Daddy'. I cannot wait to meet you." I sealed the card and the positive test and went to see him to tell him this amazingly joyous news.

"Hello, my love." I said to Andrew as I walked up to him as he was taking a small break from his duties.

"Hey babe." He said, excited to see me.

"This is for you, sweet man." I stated with a smile I held back from being too big as to not give away what the envelop contained.

He ran his finger along the seal of the envelope and pulled out the card and the positive test.

His eyes skimmed the card what looked like a few times, probably to let the text sink in. Then after a few moments of processing, the words he took in began to seep back out his eyes in wet drops that rolled down his cheeks.

"Really?" He whispered as a word made its way from his chin back to the card.

I smiled the giant smile that I was previously trying to contain and nodded my head.

He was elated, I was deliriously jovial, and we could not wait to tell the world that I was with child. The very first thing the next morning we called my mother to tell her that the Lord had given Andrew and I this child I had hoped, dreamed and prayed for, for many years.

It felt so good to tell people I was pregnant and not have to whisper it in embarrassment or try to conceal my growing bump for as long as clothing would allow. I told anyone willing to listen that I was expecting, and I wore cute, tight maternity clothes to show off my baby bump. I no longer felt like the mule with the crimson belly. I felt like I was full of life and love, not just because of the life growing in my womb, but because I was absolutely filled with the joy of the Holy Spirit.

While I understood the joy in this pregnancy, I also understood a dreaded question was coming my way.

"Is this your first?"

How would I respond to that question? Would I be denying Iris if I said yes, but would I be putting my heart in the line of fire if I said no?

After praying about where I should land on my response, I decided that I owed no person outside my doctor an explanation of my sexual/maternal history. I decided my go to answer was, "Yes, this is our first." And this child was the first Andrew and I are having together so I did not feel like I was lying.

Being prepared allotted for no awkward pauses as I decided what to say, but I was open for the Holy Spirit to prompt me to share my story with someone who was needing to hear it.

Another conversation I dreaded was telling my husband's family that Andrew's child is not my first born. I was so overcome with fear that my in-laws would disown me as their daughter-in-law. They all were very kind to me, never giving me a reason to have this intense fear but knowing the incorrect connotations the world holds about birth moms I did not want to risk having people I love condemn me in a time that I wanted to treasure. Andrew understood my reasoning and supported my decision to wait to tell his family about Iris. He held my hand then and promised me that when the time felt right, if I wanted him with me as I told them, he would hold my hand then too.

This pregnancy was my recompence for not giving up and working hard to move forward with my grief; my Galatians 6:9. Some women in my shoes try for another child soon after they place for adoption. They are grieving the loss of their birth child so deeply and do not receive the proper support to not give in to the temptation of having another child to delude the pain. I understood that mind set of having another child to alleviate the pain; even though I did have the proper support I was tempted to give in so many times, to obtain another child to make this sorrow disappear.[3] But I knew another child would never *replace* Iris and it was not fair to put so much pressure on a tiny, innocent life to be my savior. Only leaning hard into God along with my support system and intentional work on my spiritual, physical, mental, relational, financial and emotional health would help me work through the depression that I felt after placement. Administering whole-health-self-care, community care, Andrew and a whole lot of grace, forgiveness and hope from God is what got me through the hard and heavy emotions of the grief cycle.

---

[3] Please do not misread my intended meaning—not *all* pregnancies soon after placement are an effort to comfort pain. Further, every child is inherently valuable and ordained by God, no matter the circumstances around their conception.

"but God has surely listened and has heard my prayer. Praise be to God, who has not rejected my prayer or withheld his love from me!"

Psalm 66:19-20

Chapter 16

The Lord Heard
2009

My mother was there for me—like she always was. She sat on the blue plastic Doctor's office chair next to my husband, who sat beside me, holding my hand. The three of us, as patient as we could be, waited for the ultrasound technician to butter my belly and reveal the treasure inside.

Boy or girl, I was thrilled to be my baby's mommy, but my husband, my mother, the Lord and I knew that the desire of my heart was to be the mommy of a little girl.

I prayed to the Lord so many times to please let me have a daughter, please let me experience what I lost years ago. That prayer was not deviant from my heart at this moment, lying on the exam table, but it also accompanied a prayer of guarded grief.

Yes, I was thrilled to be pregnant and I was so wildly in love with this child no matter his/her gender, but I knew I needed to place the desire of my heart into the Lord's care and not allow it to become my master. I did not want to grieve the loss of a daughter in gaining a son. I wanted to be nothing but grateful and joy-filled over this precious life that God blessed Andrew and I with.

I squeezed Andrew's hand a bit tighter as the cold lubricant hit my raised abdomen. Tears began to puddle in the corner of my eyes as the technician swayed the ultrasound wand back and forth and I could see our child sweetly growing inside.

"Do you want to know what you are having?" The technician asked as she stopped the wand over our baby's legs?

"Yes, please!" I said with gusto, not taking my eyes off of the screen and praying, silently, one last time for my joy to overwhelm me, no matter the outcome.

The technician wiggled the wand around to get the small being to cooperate, so that she could inform us if we have a tiny he or bitty she sweetly growing inside.

"It's a girl!"

My mother, my husband and I holding one another's hands all looked at each other and just cried. The Lord had heard the desire of my heart and granted it to me. All my hopes and dreams that I sacrificed for Iris will now be granted to me in this tiny, precious girl. I was elated. Absolutely joy-filled, I found no other response appropriate than to cry.

Two months after the appointment that revealed I was having a girl, my mother, sister-in-law and my best friend threw a baby shower. A celebration of my daughter and me; a celebration that I did not experience with Iris, nor do I feel that I should I have. Baby showers are for mommies and with Iris I was not a mommy. But now, with Kaylin I got my chance to celebrate becoming a parent, my chance to be a *mommy*.

The shower was beautiful, pink and as you may have guessed, littered with butterflies. It was a perfect celebration of joy and life that I had always desired. God was granting me every good and perfect gift that comes from above. He granted me the love of my family, my daughter, Kaylin growing in my tummy and my ever-changing heart, morphing into the mother and the woman God had always planned me to be.

It took me years of heart ache, loss and working through grief to get to that baby shower, but I was, in a way, glad that God allowed all the mess and pain to give me this deep seeded gratitude for all that I had. Not that I was glad that Iris had the trauma of loss through adoption, but that my own trauma had brought about such growth towards God and goodness in me and my environment. I pray that Iris is able to work through her own grief for God's glory and her health as well.

I thought of Iris that special day. At this point in my life I thought of her *occasionally*, not all consuming as it used to be. I had moved forward from the constant sorrow. I was flourishing, just as I had hoped she would in my decision to place her with a well-equipped family and environment. I thought of her in how she may be so proud of me for waiting to fulfil my dream of having a family. That I married, and I was so happy. What a beautiful gift to give my birth child—a happy, mentally healthy birth mom. Even if I never meet her this side of Heaven, I knew I wanted to have my life in order, to be doing well and to be well adjusted, not stuck grieving the loss of her and my parenthood over her for the rest of my days. What a burden that would be for my child to bear. I did not want Iris to be weighed down by my grief, so I worked hard to give her a different future life on my end, even if our reunification never came to fruition, even if Iris never benefited from my betterment, my Andrew, my Kaylin and I certainly have.

Visions of joy not distorted by time displayed
in mundane and sublime.

God's faithful love does verify

in this child, my prayer, my heart's outcry.

Chapter 17

Dreams from My Past
Present Day

Back to my Kitchen

I stopped daydreaming of the past that brought me to this point in my life and calmed the hand whisking the ingredients in the bowl that was still firmly tucked to my side.

"Do you know how important you are to me?" I sincerely asked Kaylin, while also praying these words were known by Iris.

Kaylin lowered her Sippy cup and it squeaked as it refilled with air.

"Yes." She said in her tiny two-year-old voice.

Her eyes turned into downward-curving slits when she smiled big, just like mine do. She then promptly ran to me, wrapped her arms around my leg and squeezed.

I placed the mixing bowl on the counter, loosened her grip and knelt down to meet her gaze.

"Do you know how much I love you?"

At this being said, Kaylin did not answer me with her words. Instead, her eyes smiled almost bigger than her mouth and her arms swung around my neck.

"Tiiiiiiiigggggghhhhhhtttttt!" She bellowed, as if I did not already know she was squeezing me as tight as her little arms could.

For so long I dreamt of baking Christmas cookies, snuggling by the peaceful beauty of a warmly lit Christmas tree, giving tight hugs and kissing cheeks and other wonderful bonding activities a mommy does with her baby. All dreams that I sacrificed for Iris and dreams that were coming to life through the blessing of Kaylin; my sweet Kay bear, my little cricket, *my* baby girl.

Tears began to crowd my eyes and overflow down my cheeks.

"Mommy sad?" Kaylin sweetly questioned at the sight of my tears.

"No baby girl, Mommy isn't sad. Mommy is crying happy tears, because I love you and Iris so much."

I pulled her closer and squeezed her tight. Once we let go of our embrace, I picked her up, placed her on the countertop and got back to mixing the Christmas cookies my momma heart had always dreamed of...

"Now to him who is able to do immeasurably more than all we ask or imagine, according to his power that is at work within us, to him be glory in the church and in Christ Jesus throughout all generations, for ever and ever! Amen."

Ephesians 3:20-21

Chapter 18

A Few Years More...

I gathered my books from the University desk and tucked them neatly into my backpack and headed out of my class to start back home, about half a mile walk off campus.

My mother was watching Kaylin, who was now seven, and her two brothers—three-year-old Nathan who looked like my twin and six-month-old, Ethan, who also favored me—while Andrew worked, and I went to class to earn my Social Work degree.

Walking the side roads, I pinned in my phone's code and hopped onto my social media account.

Iris Lovette. I typed into the search bar. I clicked on her name and there she was. This beautiful young lady with blond hair and blue-grey eyes. A wave of thankful praise filled my Spirit as I treasured on how much my Kaylin favored Iris.

"I love you." I whispered in the depths of my heart as I slipped my phone into my back pocket to reach for my porch door.

Reeeeeeeeeeeek.

The back-door's springs announced my entry before I had the chance.

"How was class?" My Mother shouted from the front room as she was being jungle-gymmed by her three-year-old Grandson.

I placed my bookbag in the coat closet with a thud and replied, "Hi Mom, it was great. Thanks for watching my Boogaloos!"

My mom smiled brightly as she grabbed Nathan to pin him down for a belly tickle. High pitched screams of joy came barreling out from the toddler she had trapped under her forearm.

"Oh, I suffered the whole time watching my Grands." My mom said, with wide eyes as she grinned even bigger at her sarcastic remark.

I chuckled at my mom's joy for my children and turned to my sweet Kaylin Jane who was looking at a picture book on the couch.

"Kaylin, my love, let's get you to school."

She put down her book and picked up her pink backpack and her lunch box decorated with bright purple butterfly stickers. As she gathers her items I picked up my tan faux leather bag sitting by the couch.

"Mom, I'll be back after my meeting. Thanks again for watching the boys."

I kissed Nathan and Ethan on the forehead and told them both to make sure Grandma behaves while mommy is gone. To which Nathan laughed and gave his Grandma a skintight, body shaking hug.

Kaylin and I walked to the garage, hand in hand, breaking our grasp so she could hop into the back seat of the van. She buckled herself in as I climbed into the driver's seat and tossed my work bag onto the adjacent captain's chair. I fastened my own restraint, placed the gear shift into reverse and backed down the driveway to head to Oreplain Elementary, to the drop-off line.

As I pulled into the line of cars in front of the school, my bag spilled out its contents onto my passenger seat. I quickly gathered the disorder of books, papers and pamphlets and placed it neatly back inside my bag then peeked through the rearview mirror at my sweet second grader and smiled, thinking to myself how much I love that not so tiny girl with the delicate blue grey eyes.

Before I met this wonderful child, I had pictured her to look just like me. But here was, this answered prayer with blond hair and blue eyes—the complete opposite of her brothers and me. And though she did favor my husband in her facial features, he as well had brown hair and brown eyes.

Looking in the rearview mirror at my sweet baby girl, my brain finally made the connection. Kaylin was—and is—an even *bigger* answer to prayer than if the reflection of the little girl sitting in the back seat mirrored me. The likelihood of me giving birth to two blonde-haired, blue-eyed girls was not a very large chance, yet God made these half-sisters alike. What a gift for these girls who do not look like their siblings to (hopefully) one day look upon each other and feel a deep connection. At this thought, peace overwhelmed me as we pulled up farther in the drop-off line. I clicked the button to open the sliding door and turned in my seat to face Kaylin as she was climbing out of the van.

"I love you, baby girl. Have a great day and show kindness to others!"

"I love you too, Mommy! You have a great day and show kindness too!"

I blew Kaylin a kiss as she pushed the button to close the sliding door. She caught the kiss in the air and placed it on her cheek. I smiled as I turned in my seat to shift the van into drive to pull out of the Elementary lot.

I thought on my new revelation as I made my way to the meeting across town. What a gift of peace this was for me, in such a perfect time. I was heading to a meeting to be the tear and voice quake free support to an expectant family wanting to know more about their choices, including the option of viewing the potential adoptive families pictured in the adoption profiles I had placed back in my bag just moments before.

God had, and still was, comforting me in my grief and loss through His peace and His people. He refined me through my unplanned pregnancy to be rooted in His will and not my own hedonistic pursuits, and He called me to give that very same beauty He bestowed me in my ashes to others in need of His peace and people. I am His beauty from ashes. I am His Fireweed, blooming from adversity, a display of His splendor planted in His field of grace.

> "and provide for those who grieve in Zion—
> to bestow on them a crown of
> beauty instead of ashes, the oil of joy instead of mourning,
> and a garment of praise instead of a spirit of despair. They will be called oaks of righteousness, a planting of the LORD for the display of his splendor."
>
> -Isaiah 61:3

Fireweed

Acknowledgments

LaNelle: My sweet friend, thank you for all your time and effort that you lovingly poured into this book and into me. You have forever left your *stamp* on my heart.

Laurel: I am so grateful that God placed you in my life. Thank you for teaching me the beauty from ashes concept of Fireweed during our MOPS meeting all those years ago. Your words impacted my heart so greatly that I named my book after that concept. You are a treasure of a woman and I count myself blessed to call you friend.

Christa and Stacy: Thank you for giving me avenues to which I can have my voice heard. From adoption seminars and adoption retreats to speaking with hopeful adoptive families so they can gain a deeper empathy for birth/first families.

I am so grateful that you gave me opportunities which in turn gave me courage to finally publish my heart in words.

Mom: You are my best friend and confidant. Thank you for letting me read this book to you in all its many pre-published, edited forms. For all our shared tears and joys from inside these book covers and beyond, I thank you for your love, friendship and support.

Dad: For all the love you have worked hard to show me in my language, for all the donuts and soul healing conversations and for always being my support, "willing to take a bullet" for me I thank you, Daddy. You are a good man and I treasure our now relationship.

My Family-in-loves:
Thank you for hearing my story when I was ready to share it with you and for accepting me and loving me just the same. I am so glad that when I married Andrew, I got the bonus of all of you.

All those who helped behind the scenes:
Thank you for your time and efforts in helping edit my book, make connections with other supportive people and resources and for filling my cup with so much love and encouragement. I could not have done this book without you.

Poem for My Baby Jane

Hoping, praying, many tears;
Why I'm not pregnant sets in fears.
After trying and nothing yet,
Is there something I don't get?
Two more months had come and gone,
Still no baby, but to God I hold on.
Next month comes and I pray for the best;
With tears in my eyes I take the test.
Two pink lines that indicate,
My period is going to be extremely late.
Tears and songs of praise pour out;
Sorry Lord for my humanly doubt.
Tiny kicks and your heart beat,
Embracing my belly, I can't wait to meet!
Throwing up and sever back pain,
But there is so much joy to gain.
Planning, cleaning and getting ready for you;
Showers, gifts and "stretch" marks too.
Pushing, sweating and more pain,
But it's all worth it to have my baby Jane.
Small fingers, tiny toes,
My heart's so full, yet, love still grows.
Loving you first then getting to know you,

Backwards it seems, but it's true.
We loved you before you came to be,
Loving you for always and unconditionally.
Cuddling, cooing, kicking feet,
Fuzzy hair with baby smell, so sweet.
Rolling over, standing up,
Profound movements, growing up.
Walking, running, falling down,
Kissing boo-boos, turning frowns.
Messy hair and spit up clothes,
I'm worn out and no one knows.
Thankless job that has no end;
Self-pity is my accompanied friend.
Sassing, whining, stomping feet,
"It's just a chapter," I must repeat.
Overwhelmed, tired and frustrated,
Thinking of the days your dad and I dated;
Wishing for you to grow up faster,
Longing to be my life's master.
Then a voice softly said to me,
"It's all just a chapter, soon it *all* won't be".
Then I realized and took a deep breathed in,
I was wishing my time with you to be thin.
With tears in my eyes and an aching in my heart,
I asked for forgiveness for wishing us apart.
I turned my mind and set it to be
Forever on joy to be your mommy.

I realize now this little time is fleeting,
So I choose to be the mom who prayed for our meeting.
I chose to remember in the whines and sass
That the blessing to be a mommy greatly does surpass.

Notes

Chapter 3

Stabile, Suzanne. "Type One; The Perfectionist." *ROAD BACK TO YOU*, by Ian Morgan. Cron, INTERVARSITY Press, 2016, pp. 91–109.

Chapter 5

"A Quote by Theodore Roosevelt." *Goodreads* accessed April 15, 2019. www.goodreads.com/quotes/34690-people-don-t-care-how-much-you-know-until-they-know.

Chapter 2

"Top 25 Quotes by Elisabeth Kubler-Ross (of 126) | A-Z Quotes accessed April 16, 2019. www.azquotes.com/author/8304-Elisabeth_Kubler_Ross.

Chapter 3

"Mother Teresa Quotes (Author of Mother Teresa) (Page 3 of 12)." *Goodreads* accessed April 19, 2019 www.goodreads.com/author/quotes/838305.Mother_Teresa?page=3.

Chapter 4

"Caroline Leaf Quotes (Author of Switch On Your Brain)." *Goodreads* accessed April 19, 2019 www.goodreads.com/author/quotes/773964.Caroline_Leaf.

Chapter 9

Cloud, Henry. "Boundaries Quotes by Henry Cloud." *Goodreads*, accessed June 20, 2019, www.goodreads.com/work/quotes/55483783-boundaries-when-to-say-yes-how-to-say-no-to-take-control-of-your-life.

Cloud, Henry. "A Quote from Boundaries." *Goodreads*, accesses June, 21,2019, www.goodreads.com/quotes/7586757-boundaries-help-us-to-distinguish-our-property-so-that-we.

Chapter 10

"Mother Teresa Quotes (Author of Mother Teresa)." Goodreads accessed April 16, 2019.
www.goodreads.com/author/quotes/838305.Mother_Teresa.

Chapter 11

"Top 25 Quotes by Brené Brown (of 321) | A-Z Quotes accessed April 16, 2019." AZ Quotes, www.azquotes.com/author/19318-Brene_Brown.

Chapter 12

"Earl A Grollman Quote." *AZ Quotes* accessed April 15, 2019.
www.azquotes.com/quote/1033432.

Chapter 13

"A Quote by Shannon L. Alder." Goodreads accessed April 16, 2019.
www.goodreads.com/quotes/7347146-seek-a-man-that-doesn-t-ask-you-to-prove-your.

Made in the USA
Lexington, KY
23 October 2019